Critical Caring

Critical Caring

A Feminist Model for
Pastoral Psychology

Valerie M. DeMarinis

Westminster/John Knox Press
Louisville, Kentucky

Book design by Laura Lee

Cover design by Drew Stevens
Cover illustration: The Water Lily Pond, *by Claude Monet, Musée d'Orsay, Paris. Courtesy of Superstock*

First edition

Published by Westminster/John Knox Press
Louisville, Kentucky

This book is printed on acid-free paper that meets the American National Standards Institute Z39.48 standard. ∞

PRINTED IN THE UNITED STATES OF AMERICA

9 8 7 6 5 4 3 2 1

Library of Congress Cataloging-in-Publication Data
DeMarinis, Valerie.
    Critical caring : a feminist model for pastoral psychology /
Valerie DeMarinis. — 1st ed.
        p.   cm.
    Includes bibliographical references.
    ISBN 0-664-22041-X

    1. Pastoral psychology.   2. Feminist theology.   3. Caring—
Religious aspects—Christianity.   I. Title.
BV4012.D367   1993
253.5'2'082—dc20   93-19485

Contents

Acknowledgments   xi

1. Introduction   1

PART 1

2. Responsible Scavenging and the
Work of Hermeneutics for Critical Caring   23

3. A Clinical Model of Critical Caring
for Pastoral Psychotherapy   49

PART 2

4. The Case of Heather:
Images for Silence; Images for Hope   67

5. The Case of Laura:
Responsible Anger Giving Birth to Respect   83

6. The Case of Anna:
From Confession of Sin to Confession of Faith   103

7. The Case of Beth and Gina:
When Theology Creates a Context for Terror   121

8. Closing Reflections and Additional Applications
for the Clinical Model of Critical Caring   145

Notes   151

Bibliography   157

Diagrams and Figures

DIAGRAMS

1. Pastoral Psychology as Umbrella Field
   for the Therapeutic Process of Critical Caring   9

2. Method of Investigation: The Triangle of Responsibility   25

3. Pastoral Context
   Through the Worldview of Critical Caring   39

4. Overview Perspective of Human
   Development in Light of Critical Caring   43

5. Relationship of Clinical Model
   to Hermeneutic of Critical Caring   50

6. Clinical Model of Critical
   Caring for Pastoral Psychotherapy   51

7. Model of Critical Caring Applied and
   Adapted in the Different Pastoral Contexts   148

FIGURES

1. Heather's Drawing of God with "X" Mark Over Drawing   68

2. Heather's Drawing of God as a Dancing Butterfly   79

3. Laura's Three Levels of Symbolic Reality from Her Past   90

4. Laura's Chart of Herself as a Person Worthy of Care   97

5. Laura's Chart of the Therapeutic Journey   100

6. Laura's Hope for Intimacy and
   Caring with Self, God, and Others   101

7. Gina's Image of Her Relationship to God   125

8. Beth's Image of Her Relationship to God   125

This book is dedicated to four generations of women who have provided wisdom to question and courage to pursue new answers: Mary Massaglia, Rose DeMarinis, Patricia DeMarinis Mathews, and Julia DeMarinis Giddings.

Acknowledgments

Many persons and institutions have supported this project. First and foremost, I want to express appreciation to those persons whose lives and therapeutic stories are retold in this volume. Through their permission, they allow others to read of their courage, determination, and immense creativity in using faith in the pastoral psychotherapeutic context to address psychosocial and spiritual crises and issues.

I am forever grateful to my colleagues at United Theological Seminary in Minnesota, Mary Potter Engel and Mary Bednarowski, for their support and ideas for using a feminist perspective. I am also grateful to my students at United for their response to early drafts of the clinical model. A special word of appreciation is due my colleagues in pastoral psychology, Clyde Steckel and Sharon D. Parks, for their critiques of an earlier version of this work.

My thanks are due to Barbara Brown Zikmund and colleagues at Pacific School of Religion, Berkeley, for granting me release time to work on the manuscript. To my professional colleague and clinical co-therapist, Archie Smith, Jr., I offer the highest degree of respect for his clinical genius and painstaking reading of the manuscript. The involvement of Barbara Anderson and Audrey Englert, Pacific School of Religion, appears on every page of the manuscript as they typed and retyped, edited and reedited, noted and renoted till they could recite the cases from memory.

To my colleague Göran Lantz, at Ersta Health Care Institute, Stockholm,

Sweden, I wish to express appreciation for his support of the project and careful reading of the final version of the manuscript.

I wish to express sincere appreciation for the financial support of this work through three research grant sources: the Association of Theological Schools, Younger Scholar's Grant; the American Academy of Religion Research Grant; and the Graduate Theological Union Research Grant for Doctoral Faculty. Financial support has also been provided through a Swedish research stipend from AMI (Institute for Professional Development) in Stockholm, thanks to Sten Grönvall, and through a guest research position at Ersta Health Care Institute.

To the director of Westminster/John Knox Press, Davis Perkins, is due boundless appreciation not only for his professional expertise but more importantly for his support of this volume over many years of waiting. Thanks also to Alexa Smith for her clear and careful suggestions and editing of the manuscript.

Last, but certainly not least, I wish to thank my family for their support, encouragement, assistance, and patience with me. Thanks especially are given to Jan and Julia.

CHAPTER 1

Introduction

There are times when I truly experience this work of pastoral psychotherapy as the most challenging and rewarding I have ever done. These are times when theology and religion work hand-in-hand to help people find hope and direction as they struggle with emotional and psychological issues and tensions. There are other times when I find myself almost at the edge of desperation. At these times I am caught between theological doctrines and clinical wisdom. We [pastoral psychotherapists] are often on the front lines of battle as practical theologians. We see the possibilities and the disasters of theology in people's lives. And we are often left with agonizing questions of accountability and responsibility.*

Three Opening Notes

1. There are four reasons why I have written this volume. First, as one who has faced and continues to face the struggles and challenges of working across the academic, clinical, and theoretical dimensions of pastoral psychology, I think it is important to articulate those struggles and challenges as a natural but never easily experienced part of the work we do.

---

*Opening words of the author's Clinical Address: "The Use of Religious Ritual and Symbol in Pastoral Psychotherapy with Survivors of Childhood Abuse," to the Western Region of the American Association of Pastoral Counselors, San Rafael, California, 1989.

Second, my hope here is to go beyond an articulation of the extremely interesting and sometimes desperate nature of pastoral psychology to offer a working model of Critical Caring for pastoral psychotherapy. This model is not meant as a solution to anything but rather an invitation to those in pastoral psychology and related fields of concern to do their own investigation and articulation of what pastoral psychology is and does. No other field or discipline can articulate for us the work we need to do. We must undertake this for ourselves or be willing to risk the consequences of denying our responsibility. We must, naturally, work with other disciplines and find a way to incorporate such knowledge where and when we find it. However, pastoral psychology must know what its identity is in order to translate disparate segments of knowledge into working wisdom.

Third, since pastoral psychology and its clinical expressions are undergoing critical questioning from many vantage points, the time is appropriate for those working in or related to the field to communicate new ideas, theories, methodologies, and questions. To this end I hope this volume can aid this process of communication.

Finally, and perhaps most importantly, I want to share the life stories and clinical journeys of persons who have been faced with situations that challenged their ability to care at the deepest levels and who found creative and courageous ways to use their diversified expressions of belief and trust to find realistic strategies for hope and movement. In each of these situations a theological problem emerged that challenged spiritual, psychological, and social health. Each of the persons involved had to face an existential and personal crisis in order to better understand how to name and address the situation. And as a consequence, each person found new or renewed resources through their beliefs. These stories are not extraordinary. They are stories of persons struggling with issues that occur often, across all stages of the life cycle, and across cultures and social situations. What is perhaps extraordinary is the way in which each person recognized and mobilized resources within the self and through community to make changes.

These are stories about caring. These are stories that raise the deep questions that I suspect each of us has experienced in our own context. These are stories through which the questions themselves brought new ways of thinking about caring. In this sense, they are human stories for those who have learned to trust that their questioning of faith, of religion, of theological claims, and of the value of life itself is not the end but the beginning of spiritual hope.

2. Often in this volume the terms "religion," "symbol," and "feminist" appear. Though each is defined and discussed at various points in the text, I thought it might be helpful to set a general context of usage at the very beginning. The term "religion" is being used to describe a person's belief system, the system that structures how a person perceives and expresses meaning and concern. In a work such as this there is an interest in exploring the religious dimension both theologically, in its concepts and doctrines, and also phenomenologically, in its functions and behaviors.

"Symbol" is used here to refer to the elements and dimensions of belief systems that hold multileveled meaning for the believer. Symbols and the symbolic world are understood to be a part of the phenomenon of human existence. Just as with religion and belief systems, symbols can be investigated as to their contents and functions as well.

The term "feminist" refers to a system of interpretation, analysis, and assessment that raises critical questions about issues of injustice for human beings, both women and men, and suggests critical answers for envisioning and constructing situations where empowerment and interdependence are understood as essential for human existence. Within pastoral psychology, this envisioning and constructing, inspired by a feminist methodology, needs to engage all persons in its design. The term "feminist" also refers historically to a concerted effort (although by no means a single, unified effort), predominantly by women, to name and address particular inequalities and the systems causing them in women's experience and thereby in human experience as well.

In light of this dimension, I have selected four case studies that involve female persons across the life cycle, across cultures, and across systems of meaning-making. However, I have found that the feminist model of pastoral psychotherapy works effectively with male persons as well. There is a reference in this volume to one such case that I hope to develop, along with others, in a future project.

3. This is a clinical volume with emphasis on the development of a clinical model and the application of that model in four case studies. However, this is a volume that, because it is clinical, devotes a significant portion of discussion to matters of theory, philosophy, and theology. In order for a clinical volume to be sound, it must articulate the foundation of its clinical model. If it cannot do this, and be open to critical questions of theory and interpretation, then it is less than clinically responsible and potentially quite dangerous. To ignore the philosophical, theological, theoretical, or clinical dimensions of pastoral psychology is not an option for pastoral psychotherapists. I hope that this volume may further this multilevel conversation.

Having stated this, I am also aware that people approach topics from different vantage points. This makes sense although it is not often noted or valued in the way academic manuscripts are constructed. I have tried to construct this so that the reader can enter from the vantage point that makes the most sense. Though the parts of the volume are, I hope, coordinated and logically developed, it is nevertheless possible to engage another logic and move from the cases themselves back through the other parts of the volume. This is an invitation to the reader to choose a starting point of hermeneutics and theory, clinical model, or cases. After all, the evolution of the volume has followed a trajectory from therapeutic experiences and challenges, to clinical notes and questions, to an articulation of a working model, and finally to a struggling to name and articulate more precisely the foundations at work.

Structure and Presentation

The volume is divided into two parts. Part 1 focuses on the hermeneutical and theoretical task of building a foundation for understanding the meaning of caring and the process of caring in the context of pastoral psychology. This task begins here in chapter 1 as we move to understand the background and questions that led to this volume on caring and begin to explore both the nature of caring and the nature of the field of pastoral psychology through its opportunities and contexts for Critical Caring. In this chapter we will also introduce the metaphor of responsible scavenging, which will serve as a reference point throughout the volume.

Chapter 2, "Responsible Scavenging and the Work of Hermeneutics for Critical Caring," focuses on the need for and the development of a hermeneutical perspective for understanding the nature of the therapeutic encounter and that encounter in the context of pastoral psychology and pastoral psychotherapy. Through this perspective—shaped by feminist theology, feminist psychology, and the resources of pastoral care—the nature of Critical Caring is explored. Through this exploration we struggle with the questions of existence and essence, of human nature and human instinct. Finally, the chapter concludes with an overview of human development that understands Critical Caring as its center. This chapter provides the philosophical, theological, and theoretical foundations for entry into the clinical context of pastoral psychotherapy.

Chapter 3, "A Clinical Model of Critical Caring for Pastoral Psychotherapy," builds, from the hermeneutical and foundational work presented in chapter 2, a clinical model of Critical Caring and explores the clinical process involved in using the model. The clinical context of pastoral psychotherapy is discussed in terms of its unique vantage point of the pastoral perspective for therapeutic intervention and the use of the individual's religious resources in the context of a faith community.

Part 2 moves into clinical application. Chapters 4 through 7 explore the model in clinical use. Each of these chapters is devoted to one case application of the model, allowing for four very different pastoral clinical encounters. These encounters focus on the stories of females ranging in age from childhood to adulthood.

In chapter 4, "The Case of Heather: Images for Silence; Images for Hope," we are introduced to a young child struggling to spiritually and psychologically survive after a traumatic incident in her Sunday church school class where her drawing of God as male and female was crossed out because this image of God was not accepted. Heather's faith, expressed through a child's dance and imagination, enables her to look again at her drawing and confront the trauma that it caused. As healing takes place, Heather and her family undertake together the challenge of responding to the theological and life issues raised by Heather's experience.

In chapter 5, "The Case of Laura: Responsible Anger Giving Birth to Respect," we meet a young woman who is learning how to recognize responsible anger and use it as a faith resource to understand the abuse in her past. Through articulating her faith in sacred music and historical method, Laura begins to understand that she is worthy of care and that Critical Caring begins when we can name and set into perspective the painful parts of our past.

In chapter 6, "The Case of Anna: From Confession of Sin to Confession of Faith," we encounter a woman whose life is in transition and tension at every level. As she worries over the future of her children and lives with the challenges of her cross-cultural marriage, she also worries about her faith in God. Through this worry she returns with a deeper wisdom to the religious symbols and rituals of her culture. Here she finds strength to address the issues before her. This spiritual return helps Anna to distinguish her future from her past, allowing her to focus on faith instead of condemnation, and on Critical Caring instead of forced confession.

In chapter 7, "The Case of Beth and Gina: When Theology Creates a Context for Terror," we explore with Beth and Gina what it means to be estranged from a community of faith because one has a sexual orientation different from that which is accepted. Through this context of terror, Beth and Gina fight to have their relationship survive and blessed by God. Through their faith and persistence, they find a community of faith in which there is the possibility for Critical Caring.

In chapter 8, "Closing Reflections and Additional Applications for the Clinical Model of Critical Caring," discussion of the clinical application of the model of Critical Caring continues with reference to the theological and pastoral issues that have emerged through the four cases. In this chapter we come full circle to pastoral psychology as an umbrella field for Critical Caring, and we briefly discuss applications of the model in relation to the pastoral psychology continuum of care presented in chapter 1.

The Nature and Intention of This Volume

This is a manuscript about caring and how we understand patterns of care. It explores what it means to care, how our belief structure helps or hinders our ability to care, and how images of caring influence the way we learn to care or not care for ourselves and others. This discussion incorporates both theoretical and clinical dimensions of pastoral psychology.

The topic of caring and its exploration emerge out of critical reflection on the life stories of people struggling to care for themselves and others. These stories have been told and new episodes have been added to them in the clinical context of pastoral psychotherapy.

Before proceeding further, we must be clear about the context for this exploration. Two terms have been mentioned: "pastoral psychology" and "pastoral psychotherapy." Pastoral psychology denotes a field of inquiry under the larger rubric of theological investigation. However one wishes to visualize this field, as connected to applied theology or pastoral theology or some other configuration, the important point is that pastoral psychology is located within and thereby responsible to and for theology. Likewise, theology is also responsible for and to pastoral psychology.

The implications of this considerable responsibility will unfold in this volume, but it is important to understand as we begin that pastoral psychology, and therefore theology, is responsible for the theoretical orientation of the field in its approach to understanding human nature, psychosocial health and illness, and the nature and consequences of theological constructs and religious beliefs on individual and social existence. Pastoral psychotherapy is the primary clinical context for application and interpretation of the theoretical orientation of pastoral psychology. In pastoral psychotherapy the theoretical meets the actual, and through continued partnership both are enriched and refined.

Pastoral psychology is, as the name implies, a field situated in the theological context of the pastoral. It grows out of applied theology, ecclesiology, and the ecclesiastical understanding of community. It is derived to a considerable extent—although this varies within the different expressions of pastoral psychology—from the historic Christian traditions of pastoral care, the cure of souls, and the historical functions of this care.[1]

Pastoral psychology, in contemporary North American contexts, has come to include, in many of its expressions, attention to, concern for, and care of the whole person in the context of faith and the faith community. It seeks to care for persons who are understood as an integration of body, psyche, and soul. Care for the psyche and body, the person as a whole, is understood to be part of responsible care for the soul.[2] This significant and more inclusive understanding of pastoral care has many implications for the work of pastoral psychology. However, the most important implication is that the soul's health or illness must be understood in relation to the whole of a person's life and the circumstances through which meaning is made for that person in the context of culture and community.

Pastoral psychology is understood as an umbrella field for the subfields of pastoral care, pastoral counseling, and pastoral psychotherapy at the academic, theoretical, and clinical levels of engagement.[3] Each of these subfields involves a different context for caring. The contexts include different functions, lengths, and types of care, meant to address different situations and levels of caring needs. However, the foundational theological approach and the theory of care are the same in all three contexts. In other words, the argument here is that pastoral psychotherapy should be no less pastoral than pastoral care. Perhaps the kind of care needed is more intense or demands attention to deeper psychological issues in pastoral psychotherapy than in pastoral care, but these differences do not negate the need for the pastoral in both. If that adjective is functioning in a significant way, then it needs to function consistently in all three contexts. But this can only be done effectively and responsibly if pastoral psychology is clear about its nature and purpose. More will be said on this as we proceed, but now we must return to distinguishing among pastoral care, pastoral counseling, and pastoral psychotherapy.

Pastoral care is concerned with issues and events taking place in or emerging from patterns of expected progression through human development.[4] This is not to say that expectation necessarily removes anxiety concerning developmental changes, but that to some degree these transitions lie inside the realm of cultural and psychosocial consciousness. Such changes, including the natural processes of birth and death as well as all of the culturally, socially, and biologically defined events in between, have been marked by the sacramental and ritual resources of faith communities. Sacramental and ritual resources are used to address concerns raised by these changes for the individual and/or family in and through the context of the faith community. Pastoral care also involves discussion when persons are facing problems related to these life changes. Pastoral care is not merely, or should not be, the manifestation of the symbolic world of sacrament and ritual outside of a context of understanding and clarification for all participating. It is only within the context of understanding and community that the symbolic world can become manifest safely. Pastoral care is usually offered in the local church context by pastors or pastoral workers.[5]

Pastoral counseling, understood here as the second subfield of pastoral psychology, also is concerned with changes in human development. What then is the distinction between pastoral care and pastoral counseling? Pastoral counseling is needed when the limits of pastoral care have been reached. The limits are not understood as limitations but rather as indicators of a need to go further and deeper with problems, questions, and/or developmental crises in order for the person to move forward. This type of counseling usually involves short-term focus on a specific issue and work toward its resolution. Pastors and others with pastoral training work in this counseling process in the local church context or sometimes at another designated location.

The use of faith symbols, including sacraments and rituals, are also a part of the work of the pastoral counselor. However, the pastoral counselor must be able to understand and work with the individual and/or family to explore why it is and how it is that life seems, to use the words of one counselee, "just stuck in neutral like when my car stops working, and I can't get it going either backwards or forwards." The pastoral counselor works with the person or persons to define the problem and to address the concern. The pastoral counselor needs to work with the faith community's symbols to help the individual and/or family find a way through to naming and resolving the concern. In many situations this can be done well in a relatively brief period of time. In other situations the naming of the concern raises other issues, not infrequently involving some of the very symbols of the faith community that are meant to offer hope and resolution. In such situations, the levels of concern and the layers of meaning involved demand careful work by those trained to understand the complicated spiritual, psychological, and social dimensions represented. These situations are most responsibly dealt with in the context of pastoral psychotherapy.

Pastoral psychotherapy, like pastoral care and pastoral counseling, is concerned with helping persons understand and find ways to approach problems related to crises or life issues, and to use faith resources in this process. However, pastoral psychotherapy involves more intensive work with persons for whom the issues or problems cannot be resolved easily or for whom there are issues from the past that are interfering with development and action in the present. It will be argued in the next chapter that in such situations the symbolic level, including its religious representations through sacraments, rituals, and other manifestations, needs to be recognized and addressed because it holds one of the keys for release and resolution. Pastoral psychotherapy can be short-term or long-term, depending on the nature of the issues, the resources available, and the nature of the methods used in the therapeutic process. Advanced training is needed for this pastoral work, which involves coordinated academic and clinical work in theology, psychology, psychotherapy, and other areas of the social sciences. The nature and degree of coordination, especially as to the inclusion of theology and the understanding of the pastoral, are not to be assumed without careful investigation.[6]

It may be helpful to think of these subfields of pastoral psychology as situated on a continuum of pastoral caring from preventive care to intensive care. The focus on caring remains constant, but the needs are different in each case. In each of the subfields the emphasis on pastoral caring is of critical importance for survival and development. I term such pastoral caring "Critical Caring." The nature of Critical Caring will unfold in subsequent chapters. However, it is important here to understand that on the continuum of Critical Caring from preventive to intensive caring, the pastoral emphasis remains the same. It is nurtured and blooms as needed in each different context (see diagram 1).

In diagram 1, movement from left to right indicates movement from caring that is preventive and anticipatory to caring that addresses intensive problem situations. Care becomes more complex in this movement. However, the same foundation of Critical Caring undergirds pastoral care, pastoral counseling, and pastoral psychotherapy. Concern for the pastoral and the psychological are vital at each point on the continuum. As one moves right on the continuum, one brings along the dimensions of care that went before. Therefore pastoral psychotherapy also includes preventive caring as well as intensive caring, and in this regard the resources of pastoral care and pastoral counseling. The fundamental understanding of Critical Caring remains the same because the approach to human nature remains the same. Optimally, pastoral psychotherapy will foster understanding of the need for and will work to identify resources and strategies that will enable preventive caring to be a part of daily living.

In order to see the differences in these subfields of pastoral psychology, let us illustrate with a simple example. Imagine a couple preparing for marriage. The couple comes to the minister, priest, or designated pastoral caregiver for premarital sessions. In these sessions the couple is given the chance to talk about issues, raise questions, and make plans for their wedding. The

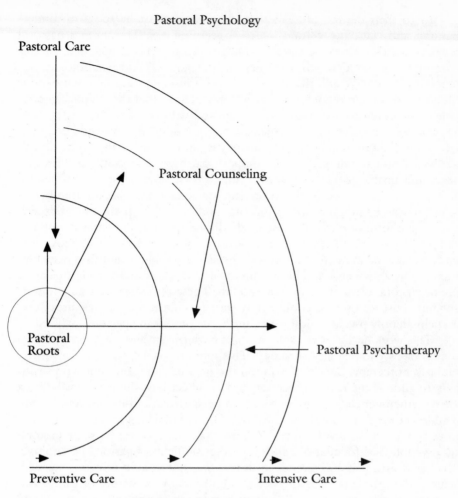

Diagram 1. *Pastoral Psychology as Umbrella Field*
for the Therapeutic Process of Critical Caring

couple asks for blessing on their plans and prayer for their future. Important issues arise, but in this situation of caring, the preventive or forward-looking dimension is dominant. The couple is there to talk about and plan for things that they anticipate and to get some ideas on how to work toward a hopeful and stable life together. This is a situation of pastoral care.

Now imagine another couple coming for premarital sessions. The same issues, questions, plans arise but in addition to this, the couple is struggling with, for example, the area of sex and sexual expression. As the pastoral care-giver talks with the couple, it becomes clear that before the couple can move forward to their desired life together, more time must be spent on understanding and clarifying certain issues concerning sex. The trained pastoral caregiver works with the couple, or finds someone who is qualified for this more intensive work, which will draw on the spiritual and psychological resources of the couple and the caregiver. In this instance pastoral counseling is able to address the more intensive needs presented so that the couple can continue in its preventive work toward a happy and stable life together.

In the third case, imagine a couple arriving quite anxious and apprehensive. Initial probing reveals that the anxiety is not only about the future and all the details of a wedding, but one or both partners seem confused, disorganized, and unable to move forward, though their desire is strong to build a life together. The cause of this more intense anxiety may be any number of things, but let us suppose that in this situation one of the partners had experienced some form of physical abuse in childhood that was only now coming to memory. In such a situation, the person may want and desire to move forward, but for the moment dimensions of the past are blocking this movement. Intensive work is needed. The resources of faith expressed through pastoral care or pastoral counseling are not enough. These resources are vitally important but must be used in conjunction with psychotherapeutic resources that can help identify psychological issues and strategies for the persons involved.

This work necessitates exploration of both psyche and soul, using the resources of psychology and theology. This intensive work, the process of pastoral psychotherapy, does not abandon the present and future but works with them to address the past. In this way, if done effectively, the person will find a way to remember the past safely, put it in perspective, and use preventive care to address the future in light of the past and present. The intensity and dimensions, though more involved in this third example, involve the same pastoral and psychological foundations as in the other subfields of pastoral psychology. In other words, it is a difference in degree and not in kind of caring needed. Central to all these fields is the need to understand the nature of caring and the essential role religious and spiritual beliefs and symbols play in the ability to care. Pastoral psychology has the unduplicated therapeutic position and access for exploring the ways in which and means by which beliefs and symbols can help with or hinder the process of Critical Caring, and for actively using these beliefs and symbols in the therapeutic context.

Assumptions in Approach to Pastoral Psychotherapy

Our focus here is on pastoral psychotherapy, where Critical Caring involves several levels of intensity. Five assumptions underlie our approach to pastoral psychotherapy. First, the therapeutic orientation to care undergirding pastoral psychotherapy involves theology working in conjunction with psychology and other disciplines. Second, pastoral psychotherapy is concerned with understanding, assessing, and incorporating the nature and role of belief, meaning-making, and symbolic action in its care of the whole person. Third, theological and ethical patterns that interrupt or harm caring need to be named and analyzed. Fourth, analysis and action at every level of the therapeutic process need to recognize and, if appropriate, involve the community (or communities) through which the person or persons make meaning. Fifth, pastoral psychotherapy is a process that takes place among persons, among therapeutic partners whose common goal is to make caring possible for self and others.

Though pastoral psychotherapy is our focus here, the questions, issues, discussion, and approach are not the property of one context, subfield, or even field. These questions, issues, discussion, and approach have emerged from critical engagement and reflection on life stories and patterns of caring with persons involved in the day-to-day challenge of trying to care about self and others. The model here presented will, it is hoped, be of use also to those professionals engaged in other branches of psychotherapy concerned with the task of caring and its relation to the nature and function of religious and spiritual belief and symbols.

Approaching Caring

Caring is as basic to life as life itself. Life is absolutely dependent on human caring. If then caring is so basic and vital to life, why is it a challenge to care? When discussing caring or any other term that signifies something vital to life, we find ourselves challenged to understand the term itself and that which it signifies. This challenge depends on many factors but the greatest is that we are always living within the term we are trying to objectify in order to explore and define it. This obviously cannot be finally accomplished. Therefore, we can explore and define caring but can never stop simultaneously living within it, and so the challenge remains.

The way we approach the term "caring" and the way we explore and define this dimension of reality will make a difference in the way we come to know and live caring. Many approaches are available, each with its own framework for understanding caring. This volume represents but one approach. Each approach has consequences. Each has a way of interpreting reality, and this interpretation makes a critical difference in the way life is approached and caring is understood and lived. If an approach to caring clearly defines its foundation and its interpretation of reality, then the consequences of the approach can be examined responsibly.

It may seem a bit unusual that the term "caring" is here paired with the term "critical." Caring and critical need each other. Both as a term and as a signifier of reality, caring has often been understood in a way that has caused dangerous and harmful consequences, leading ultimately to patterns and acts of uncaring. In order to bring attention to these consequences and to the approach to caring undergirding them, we need to identify an approach that understands caring as lifegiving and healing. "Caring" as a term needs a descriptor to distinguish health-producing caring from illness-producing caring. Both health and illness are to be understood within a cultural and community context of meaning-making.[7] Critical Caring is the term used here. More will be said shortly on Critical Caring and a feminist approach. In preparation, a background story about pastoral psychology needs to be told.

Background and Context for This Volume

Pastoral psychology and pastoral psychotherapy, the theoretical and clinical dimensions through which caring will be explored, can be understood in different ways that will lead to different consequences. Having identified pastoral psychology as an umbrella theological field for the process of Critical Caring, I think it important to relate an incident whose central image and challenge led me to think of pastoral psychology in this way.

A number of years ago, when I was a relative newcomer to the field, I overheard a conversation between two professors of systematic theology. The topic was pastoral psychology in general, and the pastoral practitioner in particular. One said to the other:

They are just like scavengers. They have no real theory, just a hunting and pecking, a grabbing and applying. There is no order for them. And they can never explain what they do or why they do it, only that something works or not. It is all technique, and at best has some rationale to measure if it works. It is a very sad state of affairs.

As one embarking on a professional career in the field of pastoral psychology I initially experienced a wide range of negative reactions to this statement. I found myself on the defensive and silently raising questions such as "What do they know about psychology or pastoral psychology?" "How can systematic theologians who work with ontology, theology, and constructs understand the complicated work of pastoral practitioners?" "Does pastoral psychology belong to theology or to psychology?"

Time passed but the comments and the image of the scavenger remained with me. Through it I found myself struggling to understand the field of pastoral psychology and its nature. In confronting the somewhat daunting image of the scavenger, three concerns for the field of pastoral psychology emerged.

First, technique understood as an end in itself is an insufficient and dangerous approach to and understanding of pastoral psychology. Neither this field nor any other in the caring professions can be engaged responsibly in its helping human beings live more responsible and caring lives if it does not struggle to articulate its approach, its philosophy of human nature, and its understanding of pain and healing. Pastoral psychology must struggle not only to articulate its operating philosophy but also its theology. Pastoral psychology belongs to the theological enterprise. It needs to own this foundation and be responsible for it and accountable to it.

Second, as a field within theology, pastoral psychology needs to engage its theological partners. It must face not only the challenges presented by the other theological fields but must challenge them as well. Pastoral psychology plays a unique role in theological investigation. Through its many means of access, it is on the front line of faith struggling to interpret theology in the everyday situations of human living and caring. This access allows for the gathering of human stories that need theology's attention and reflection. As we will explore in this volume, human stories are shaped in large measure, whether consciously or otherwise, by theology's constructs, images, and interpretations. Theology needs to understand and take responsibility for its constructs, images, interpretations, and their consequences.

Third, pastoral psychology as a field and the pastoral psychotherapist as practitioner need to identify a primary image for their theoretical and clinical work. For our purposes, I propose the scavenger as a precise and operative image. Unlike the theologian who voiced the derogatory remark concerning pastoral psychology and scavenging, I understand the image of scavenging as positive, accurate, and appropriate for the work of pastoral psychology. My proposal is that those engaged in the field of pastoral psychology *are* scavengers. We scavenge to find ways to make Critical Caring possible.

Scavengers, though often thought of negatively, are in point of fact highly skilled at collecting, extracting, and cleansing. A scavenger makes critical distinctions, judgments, and selections. Scavengers have the ability to investigate beneath the surface in order to make important decisions.[8] The denotations of the word "scavenger" do not match the connotations of the word. A scavenger has come to be associated with just one of its denotations, that of a "thief" or "user of rubbish." The scavenger becomes one who is indiscriminate, careless, and undisciplined. Scavenging can be done responsibly or irresponsibly in a given context and for a particular situation. The responsible scavenger is one skilled at survival, one who knows how to search, salvage, purify, and transform the elements of the world into that which nurtures and sustains life. The responsible scavenger can identify, discriminate between, and, through wisdom and flexibility, transform disparate kinds of knowledge into wisdom. I can think of no more precious tool than wisdom for those working in pastoral psychology. And since the image of the responsible scavenger connotes wisdom, it seems a worthy image for the field.

The theological field of pastoral psychology in its theoretical understanding and through its clinical orientation in pastoral psychotherapy has the task of Critical Caring at its center. Working with persons to care for themselves and others is a challenging opportunity for those in the clinical context of pastoral psychotherapy. Such an opportunity demands the imaginative use of resources that are theological, psychological, spiritual, social, cultural, and/or physical. At times the use and combination of these resources must be done using hunches and clues of various sorts. Though there are images and ideas about caring, there is no ideal prototype that applies to every situation and context.

Therefore, in pastoral psychotherapy, the persons involved need to find a way, in partnership, to search for, seek out, explore, evaluate, and transform what is available, or can be available, into the wisdom that will nurture caring. This is done by responsible scavenging. The pastoral partners engage in searching, salvaging, purifying, and transforming in order to heal and care. Responsible scavenging is the means to human caring, survival, and development. It offers a strategy that transforms hope into realized direction. Responsible scavenging emerges from the life-giving belief system of person in the context of community. Responsible scavenging is the art that undergirds Critical Caring. If pastoral psychology is to undertake the challenge of Critical Caring, it must learn the art of responsible scavenging.

Critical Caring Through a Pastoral Feminist Perspective

If pastoral psychology is to undertake Critical Caring through responsible scavenging, it needs first to define the term. "Critical" comes from the noun "critic," and "caring" from the verb and noun forms of "care." The two words "Critical Caring" are not often thought of together outside of the Western medical world where "critical care" indicates a life-threatening condition, a situation requiring intensive attention and care. The psychotherapeutic and pastoral communities usually have not used this term. If anything, it may seem to be a juxtaposition of conflicting ideas in the pastoral and psychotherapeutic contexts. One professional colleague observed, at seeing "Critical Caring" in reference to psychotherapy:

> Seeing critical and caring together seems strange to me. Supportive caring or just caring describes the therapeutic goal. But critical caring is so negative sounding. It smacks of judgment and forcing something. . . . Many people need therapeutic help because of all the critical messages they've been given. Why would you want to link these together?

My colleague's response and question came as no surprise. At first analysis, "critical" and "care" seem to represent opposing forces. "Critical" denotes the giving of harsh and adverse judgment, judgment that is censorious, carping, fault-finding.[9] After all, does not the word "critical" imply an insensitivity, an obvious lack or negation of caring? "Caring" denotes concern, solicitude, charge over, to provide for, to regard, to preserve.[10] Does not the idea of caring, therefore, mean that there is no room for being critical? Are they not functional opposites? The answers to these questions are understood frequently to be yes, especially when constructed on a philosophy of life that sees human isolation, apathy, and self-centeredness as the norm.

The answers to these questions are very important for understanding the nature of caring. Answering either of these questions in the affirmative is problematic. When this happens, we make separate and incompatible two functions that should be distinct but inseparable. We force apart human functions that desperately need each other for responsible survival and for responsible scavenging.

It is important to ask the question: Why have critical and caring come to be seen as functional opposites in many Western cultures? Many reasons contribute to this, but three are especially important because they emerge time and again in the clinical setting as problematic blocks to Critical Caring. First, there has been and continues to be a fully or partially conscious social pattern that associates and assigns the term "critical" to a "male" or "masculine" function and "caring" to a "female" or "feminine" one.[11] By this very assignment of critical and caring to predetermined, gender-based categories, dialogue becomes strained or nonexistent. At its best, such gender-based categorization might lead to a complementarity.[12] However, even at its theoretical best, this assignment is functionally problematic. Critical needs caring and caring needs critical in *each* human decision. Splitting these functions by gender results in an inability of any person, whether male or female, to use the functions conjointly either intrapersonally or interpersonally.

This assigning process leads to a second reason for understanding critical and caring as opposites and that leads consequently to a second problem: the problem of power and powerlessness, voice and voicelessness. Critical is perceived as powerful, and power is viewed as a function that discriminates unmercifully. This kind of power works to delineate and destroy. It is competitive and destructive, not cooperative. Caring is viewed, on the other hand, as merciful but essentially powerless. It comes into play *after* critical has done its job. It remains in the background picking up the pieces, perhaps suggesting clues for criticizing destructive power, but essentially without a voice and certainly without influence to alter existing power structures. Just as power is built on the assignment of gender-specific functions to caring and critical, so the third reason and resulting problem are built upon the second, the defining of power.

Third, there is a framework of thought that considers human nature to be dominated by isolation and distance. Shared power and partnership are viewed as unnatural. Thus a defensive posture is essential for the self's survival. Relationality and cooperation are not understood as basic to human nature. Human nature must work against its natural tendencies in order to be relational. The self is not by conscious nature or development relational, but by nature and instinct strives to dominate the other.[13] One self is in competition with another. Ironically, although human beings in infancy and throughout life are vitally dependent on caring for survival, the critical function is more commonly stressed as the key to human achievement in this way of perceiving human reality. The critical function enables distance and separation, securing the perpetuation of aloneness and the spread of pathology. Caring is seen as naturally inferior to the critical function. As such it is applied to those who, by category, are also understood to be in an inferior position. This categorization often follows gender-asymmetrical patterns; men engage in the critical function and women engage in the caring function. In the end, however, the critical function *needs* to dominate the caring function because that is how human nature is perceived.[14]

The life patterns developed when critical and caring are perceived to be functionally disoriented toward communication or to be logically incapable of communication are not healthy or responsible survival patterns. They do not lead to human behavior that is cooperative and nurturing to self and others. They consume an excessive amount of human energy in "suspicious survival,"[15] survival that is terrified of trust, that holds little hope for the future, and that is often terrorized into immobility.

The present work attempts to bring critical and caring into dialogue in order to create a working model of Critical Caring for pastoral psychology. Having seen the definitions of critical and caring above, the reader is quite reasonably wondering why anyone would wish to engage in such a dialogue. After all, if critical is essentially destructive and caring primarily addresses a situation of need, often leading to overprotection and lack of functioning, what would be the purpose of bringing them into dialogue? What could anyone hope to gain by such an enterprise?

The answer is straightforward: nothing. If one attempts to dialogue with the above definitions of caring and critical operating, there will be no possibility for dialogue. Critical tears down; caring desperately attempts to protect and shelter. The definitions lock the functions in a vicious cycle of antagonism from which there is no escape. The two functions need to be redefined.

Further investigation reveals other possibilities. Care does denote mental suffering, sorrow, grief, and trouble, a burdened state of mind linked to fear, doubt, or concern. However, care can also be defined as appropriate interest and concern, taking caution in avoiding harm or danger. Care has medical associations in its reference to attending to the sick, but care is not related to the Latin *cura*, to cure. Critical, likewise, has other denotations. It means the ability to make careful and skillful judgments. In its medical associations it means: of or relating to a crisis in the sense of a decisive moment, a crucial moment.[16]

One may do well to wonder about denotations for the same term that signify crucially different meanings. As so often occurs in human conversation, the same word may be used by different people with very different understandings of what it means. Because the clarification of meanings goes largely unexplored, conversation ends in miscommunication. The hope for dialogue is lost. Definitions of terms and their applications are crucial for dialogue. As concerns "critical" and "caring," however, these other denotations offer not only hope for dialogue but a crucial partnership. Let us first approach dialogue.

The prior juxtapositioning of the terms "critical" and "caring" is based on the nature of definitions given to each word and the cultural connotations associated with each. The transition from juxtaposition to dialogue mandates two actions: first, a change of definitions for *each* term, and second, a concerted openness to dialogue between the terms. Understanding the crucial connection between dialogue and definition allows one to recognize the potential for miscommunication when significant terms that have polyvalent meanings are left undefined. Examining why dialogue is or is not taking place by exploring functioning definitions is a method of exploration built on a philosophy whose goal is communication. Only through dialogue can change take place at the foundation of communication, that of naming and ordering. This approach understands that the denotations and connotations of terms are built on many layers of explication and interpretation. If change is to take place, then the significance of naming and ordering the universe becomes heightened for all partners in the dialogue. This will be further discussed as part of our hermeneutical analysis.

Returning to "critical" and "caring," we need a way of identifying these terms for our use if dialogue between them is to be possible. "Critical" is to be understood both as careful judgment and crucial intervention. Both definitions are needed to link thought and action. "Caring" is to be understood as appropriate concern. Dialogue between critical and caring as identified in this way can lead to a working partnership between them that claims responsibility for the construction of a model of Critical Caring for pastoral psychology.

Critical Caring signifies, therefore, the ability for careful judgment and appropriate concern to work together for crucial intervention. A model of Critical Caring for pastoral psychology takes belief systems seriously, works to understand their impact on naming and ordering the universe, and assesses their interaction with Critical Caring. To build this model, we need a theological foundation and an operative psychoanthropological theory. This brings us to feminist theory and a pastoral feminist perspective.

A Pastoral Feminist Perspective

Pastoral psychology requires a theological foundation and operative psychoanthropological theory that appreciates and incorporates a dialogue between critical and caring, leading to a model of Critical Caring. There are four reasons why feminist theology and feminist psychosocial theory can be used as a foundation for a model of Critical Caring for pastoral psychology. The term "Feminist," of course, has a variety of denotations and many more connotations. "Feminist" describes both a philosophy and a process. Central to both is an understanding that each human being is entitled to care, respect, and dignity by the fact of their humanity.

Human nature is meant to be lived in and through caring and responsible relationships. A feminist perspective recognizes that women and other groups of persons often have not been treated humanely and have often been denied the respect and dignity to which human beings are entitled. Consequently, the critical questions of a feminist approach serve to assess the consequences of a philosophy of human nature that denies caring and responsible relationship. Such a philosophy cannot understand Critical Caring and does not offer voice or power to women and other persons regarded by such a philosophy as less than deserving, able, or entitled to have voice or access to power. Such a categorization process essentially designates these persons as being less than human.

The spiritual, psychological, and social consequences of this process are very serious. The assessing of consequences is coupled with critical questioning that works to envision responsible and realistic possibilities of hope for the present and future. The assessing and envisioning functions of critical questioning from a feminist perspective begin with the assumption that neither human health nor human illness can be investigated accurately by looking at the human being in isolation. Critical questions must be directed toward both the intrapersonal and interpersonal dimensions of health and illness. The feminist perspective used here includes first, an understanding of human life as a process of relationship dependent on caring for self and others in the context of community; second, a critical analysis of women's needs and female developmental issues within a cultural context of a nonrelational and noncaring value system; and third, a means of assessing the negative impact of this cultural context on all persons in the culture, female and male, and on the caring process among persons.

With this orientation to the meaning of the term "feminist," we can proceed to the four reasons why feminist theology and psychosocial theory provide a unique and suitable resource for pastoral psychology.

First, feminist theology and feminist psychosocial theory challenge us to recognize the need to investigate carefully what is at the surface, and what is at the core of beliefs, symbols, assumptions, and categories of meaning-making. Discernment is the most vital dimension of the critical function. Feminist resources also offer the challenge of recognizing the need for nurture, the need to offer sustenance for growth and development of the whole person in the context of community. Nurture is the most vital dimension of the caring function.

Second, feminist psychosocial theory and theology offer access to the wisdom coming from voices challenging existing perceptions across disciplines, voices that need to be heard by those concerned with pastoral psychology.[17]

Third, both feminist theology and feminist psychosocial theory understand belief systems and their influence to be an essential part of the way human life and relationships come to have meaning. What we believe in and the symbolic constructions of our world influence the way we think, feel, and act. Within a feminist framework, both theology and psychology begin with a respect for and a need to include religious belief and spirituality in the understanding of psychosocial health and healing. Likewise, both understand that religious belief and spirituality also must take responsibility for their role in psychosocial pathology and illness. Feminist theology and feminist psychosocial theory are not at odds with or in competition with each other. They are and need to be companions in dialogue if health and healing through Critical Caring are the desired goals.

Fourth, feminist theology and psychosocial theory incorporate a praxis methodology, which demands that action and reflection work in tandem. This allows for questioning and examining both outside and inside a particular theory or field. Theory itself is viewed as a prototype rather than archetype for it must also be open to critical questioning and change.[18] The ability to question and listen as well as speak and name reveals a pattern in which both the caring and the critical functions operate.

Feminist theology and feminist psychosocial theory are the products of deliberate critical and caring questioning. They, as fields of investigation, have been born out of passion and intellect working in dialogue to name the consequences that result from an inability to frame and raise critical and caring questions. Pastoral psychology's task of responsible scavenging, built on a feminist theological and psychosocial foundation, requires coordination at the theoretical, academic, and clinical levels. Through this coordination a model of Critical Caring can be developed from the insights and questions raised at each level. It is to this task of responsible scavenging that we will proceed.

PART 1

PART I

CHAPTER 2

Responsible
Scavenging
and the Work
of Hermeneutics
for Critical Caring

This chapter is concerned with building a functioning hermeneutic for pastoral psychology, by which the nature of human nature is explored and upon which a clinical model of Critical Caring can be built. Responsible scavenging by way of and through feminist theology and feminist psychosocial theory will provide pivotal resources for this building process.

Pastoral psychology and pastoral psychotherapy, like other psychological and psychotherapeutic orientations, are appropriately understood as founded on philosophy and on science. Perhaps the philosophical foundation is the more essential for our focus since it shapes the direction of how research questions are selected, which questions are asked, and how results are interpreted. This is not to say that science has no significant place in this work nor to eschew the necessity for empirical research. But it is to say that the work of the therapeutic process emerges from a set of values and assumptions about the nature of life, human instincts, health, hope, and illness. The therapeutic process exists within an interpretive framework and cultural context.[1]

Philosophical exploration of the value system of a therapeutic orientation is essential for an in-depth understanding of that system. Before we examine the working theory being used in this therapeutic context, it is important to investigate the theory's underlying philosophical assumptions. Therefore an investigation of philosophy needs to come before an examination of theory. This investigation involves a hermeneutical inquiry into the foundation upon which operating theory and clinical models are built.[2]

A hermeneutical investigation can be done from many perspectives. The perspective influences the questions raised and the categories involved. As one engaged in responsible scavenging, I have experimented with and tested many different perspectives. The questions and categories of investigation offered by a feminist perspective are important for pastoral psychology. Therefore, my choice is a feminist perspective constructed with reference to the works of theological and biblical scholar Elisabeth Schüssler Fiorenza and clinical psychologist and psychosocial theorist Susan Sturdivant. Through the scavenging process, I have found dimensions of each scholar's work to be significant and relevant for pastoral psychology. Their works provide resources and reference points.[3]

The feminist perspective offered here provides a means of investigation that we will refer to as the Hermeneutic of Critical Caring. The investigation may be thought of as a type of scavenging journey. It involves a process of movement, with each step adding different dimensions. Our investigation involves four steps. First, we will introduce the method of investigating at work here, the method that we call the Triangle of Responsibility. Second, we will examine the foundation of this method, the base of our Triangle of Responsibility. It contains the theological and psychological values and worldview that determine the nature of life, human instincts, health, illness, and hope. This foundation provides the most important part of the hermeneutic of Critical Caring, for it determines what happens in the theoretical and clinical dimensions of the therapeutic. Third, we will set the hermeneutic of Critical Caring into the field of pastoral psychology. And in the fourth and final step we will visualize our pastoral feminist perspective through a model of human development. At the end of our scavenging journey, we will be prepared to move into the clinical model of Critical Caring, which is the subject of chapter 3.

Step 1. Method of Hermeneutical Investigation: Triangle of Responsibility

> Central to every form of psychotherapeutic treatment are beliefs about what people are like and what they might become, as well as a conceptual framework within which to order and understand the data of human experience and behavior.[4]

If we agree with Susan Sturdivant's starting point, then we need to approach our exploration with an awareness that therapeutic and psychotherapeutic interventions are based on certain values, perceptions, and worldviews.[5] We begin by asking questions to ascertain the functioning values and operative worldviews influencing the given theory. Before questions can be asked, we need to know the levels we are investigating. We need to distinguish three levels to which questions can be posed: (a) philosophy, (b) theory, and (c) technique. Sturdivant distinguishes among them as follows:

Philosophy of treatment becomes the examination of the belief system underlying a given type of therapy, as well as the implications of the beliefs and values for the practice of that therapy. This is as distinguished from *theory*, which is defined as assumptions and evidence about personality dynamics (that is, how people work both intrapsychically and interpersonally); and from *techniques*, which are specific interchanges between therapist and client designed to facilitate reaching therapeutic goals.[6]

Those of us working in pastoral psychology must make an immediate adjustment to Sturdivant's levels by adding theology as the partner to philosophy at the foundational level of exploration.[7] By doing so, we transform Sturdivant's design in an unalterable way. Responsible scavenging requires us to do so if we claim our foundation in pastoral psychology. However, the function of the levels remains the same. Theology and philosophy remain the foundation for theory and technique. Theology's worldview shapes philosophy, and philosophy's categories influence theological reflection. These in turn shape theory and technique. The following is my diagrammatic interpretation of Sturdivant's categories translated and revised for pastoral psychology and the pastoral practitioner, and named the Triangle of Responsibility (see diagram 2). The term "responsibility" is used for three reasons. First, it signals that there is an important function to be performed. Second, it locates this function in the domain of the academic and clinical professionals responsible for assessment and care delivery, giving them the responsibility for investigating theological and philosophical assumptions. Third, it is meant to bring attention to the issue of internal consistency within the triangle. The levels need to be coordinated with one another.

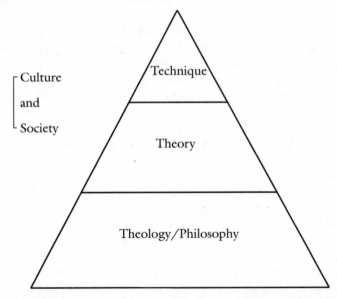

Diagram 2. Method of Investigation: The Triangle of Responsibility

The Triangle of Responsibility is built in three levels. The bottom level provides the foundation. Though there is movement and interaction within and among the different levels, primary movement is upward from the foundational level. In this way, the bottom level is responsible for that which is built upon it. Questions that may arise concerning theory, the understanding of intrapersonal and/or interpersonal structures, or psychopathology do not get answered thoroughly at the theoretical level. These questions raise issues and concerns at a deeper level. Such questions, therefore, need to be examined at the level of theological and philosophical values and belief structures.

For instance, let us suppose that we encounter a theoretical construct that states that healthy women's development is *dependent* on the fulfillment of the biological, emotional, and theological need to bear and nurture a child. This construct as construct is clear and precise. Therefore, it is logical that any woman who does not have this need or chooses not to understand it as a need or who is unable to fulfill the need must be problematic and pathological. When we set a living human being in the context of a theoretical construct from which there are no variations, any variation in the human expression must logically be labeled a problem. If we begin and end at the level of theory in our exercise here, and call that theory scientific and thereby unquestionable, then there is no recourse but to understand that there is a problem and that the problem resides in the individual woman. The case is closed to critical questions and consequently to critical options.

However, if we understand that theoretical constructs are built on values and belief structures and are influenced by cultural and social structures, we create an option for examining both theory and living situations that appear to be in tension with theoretical assumptions. We then have the human opportunity and professional obligation to examine carefully the operative theory and the theological and philosophical base on which it is constructed. In this example, investigating at the bottom level, theology and philosophy, might eventually lead us to find the following truth claims, those beliefs and assumptions most basic to the structure and construction of worldview: women are willed by God to bear children; women find happiness through dependency relationships; women are less able to function using reason; women are by nature caring of others and need to express this care toward children; and a woman who does not understand her true nature is both spiritually and psychologically ill and dangerous.

In this example the theological and philosophical base of the triangle contains truth claims, which in turn form the operative worldview. Theoretical formulations are built on the truth claims and worldview of the theological and philosophical base. This is the interpretive structure, the essential hermeneutical level. It is to the depths of this level that we must go if change is to occur at the theoretical level. Definitions of health and illness are based on the interpretations of life, truth, and the ordering of reality grounded at this deep hermeneutical level. The other levels in the Triangle of Responsibility will be discussed in chapter 3 through the presentation of the clinical model of Critical Caring. The Triangle of Responsibility can be used to investigate any theory and the worldview on which it is constructed. Clinicians and professionals within the field of pastoral psychology, or for that matter most other psychotherapeutic orientations, may at first perceive this method of investigation to be above and beyond the limits or scope of their work. However, it is precisely this perception that is being challenged here. We who are concerned with and engaged in this work have an obligation to ourselves and those with whom we work to do this kind of investigation. If our training and academic work have not adequately prepared us to do this or have fostered a negative incentive against this kind of inquiry, we must find a way to overcome these obstacles. This is a responsibility we have and one that only we can undertake.

Step 2. The Hermeneutic of Critical Caring

We move now from a general description of the investigative method of the Triangle of Responsibility to an application of this method in a particular hermeneutical orientation, that of Critical Caring. Within the hermeneutic of Critical Caring, investigation of the bottom level of the Triangle of Responsibility reveals the operative truth claims and worldview.

Before proceeding further with an analysis of this particular worldview, we need to understand what is at stake in a discussion of worldview. Historian of religion Ninian Smart offers a helpful way of understanding the term "worldview." A worldview "must make some reference to what folks feel, the ideas they have, the structures of belief of their society—in a word, to human consciousness."[8] Worldview is a whole in itself. Deciphering its dimensions is a complex activity since a worldview encompasses how life, the world, and even the universe are ordered. A worldview consists of scientific facts, cultural interpretations and categories, and truth claims about the essence and existence of human beings. The hermeneutical foundation of a worldview can be compared to a functioning paradigm that determines the perception of and approach to reality. Scholars, theoreticians, and clinicians use paradigms and must understand their function as "a disciplinary matrix [that] determines the acceptable theoretical models, permissible ideologies, heuristic concepts that assign weight and priority to agreed-on beliefs as well as organize diverse information, 'facts,' and 'data' in a coherent interpretative framework."[9]

A hermeneutic of Critical Caring means that the worldview in operation is one that makes Critical Caring possible. What makes Critical Caring possible? To answer this most basic question, we are brought immediately to the fundamental topic of human nature. How we approach this topic determines virtually everything else, or at least that which concerns health, illness, pathology, and the nature of the therapeutic. The importance of the topic of human nature demands a stark and clear approach.

Critical Caring understands human nature as instinctual. The very word "instinctual" is neither popular nor positive in many contemporary therapeutic contexts.[10] Connotations of morbid and/or uncontrollable dimensions of human beings abound when the term "instinct" is invoked.[11] Yet the term itself is important and needs to be reclaimed. Instinct denotes natural or spontaneous inclinations or tendencies in human beings, that which is innate and basic to human nature. Instinct can also be defined as that which is charged with life, such as a moving or animating force or principle.[12] Instinct is that aggregate of unlearned responses that identifies a species. Instinct therefore does not require the exercise of reason.[13]

The term "instinct" need not be associated with the morbid or uncontrollable, and it need not be placed in opposition to reason. Through responsible scavenging, "instinct" can be reclaimed and refined. Instinct represents a species' basic dimension of response and survival. Instinct contains the coding for understanding a species. Instinct is like a field of energy that manifests itself through the context and resources surrounding human life. We cannot afford to abandon or ignore instinct because it is too basic to human nature. Awareness of human instinct is essential to understanding Critical Caring. A lack of awareness of human instinct contributes to psychosocial pathology because pathology flourishes when basic instincts are not understood.

Societal, spiritual, psychological, and physical dimensions of health necessitate the acknowledgment, understanding, and responsible nurturing of instincts. Societal, spiritual, physical, and psychological manifestations of illness are exacerbated by conscious or unconscious attempts to confuse, alter, or block the instincts. The force necessary to create illness is immense for it must captivate imagination, reason, and energy. Such force is accompanied by an operative worldview. Through worldview a functioning hermeneutic is created by which reality is named and ordered. If the worldview does not understand the nature and needs of the instincts, it will create its own truth claims that work against the instincts. This is how societal, spiritual, and psychological illness is created and sustained.[14]

If human nature is instinctual, we must then proceed to name and understand the human instincts. The scavenging process undertaken at the clinical and theoretical levels has led to the identification of two instincts central to human nature and critical for human health: the relational instinct and the religious instinct.

Clinically and theoretically, the identification of the religious and relational instincts can be traced through three phases of development. Before becoming theoretically informed of the philosophical and value-laden foundation of psychotherapeutic systems, I became clinically aware. My early clinical work took place in Freudian and neo-Freudian environments. I became aware of the manner in which religious and/or symbolic material was interpreted. These environments were at a certain loss to understand this material in a constructive manner. When clients themselves expressed directly or indirectly how life-giving their symbolic experiences and religious experiences were, the interpretive framework seemed at a loss to hear them. However, when clients talked about their negative symbolic experiences, the framework of interpretation seemed to accommodate this material much more easily. To put it mildly, it seemed that entire areas of thought and action dealing with the symbolic were being interpreted through an elaborate system of reconfiguration. This was puzzling to me and often confusing if not debilitating to the clients involved.

Though I did not understand fully at the time, I was experiencing a worldview in action. Only much later in my clinical and academic work did I become acquainted with metapsychology and its tools of analysis. This helped me understand that the framework of interpretation shaping my training experience was built on a theory that essentially and functionally considered human nature to be the product of an uncontrollable primary instinct, id, which needs to be held in check. Such a warring metaphor left little room for cooperative instincts working within or between persons. As philosopher and clinician Eugene Gendlin has noted, the id

> consists in merely individual, chemical drives, tension-increases or decreases. It gets order only from interactions which are patterned by the existing society through the ego. . . .
> In Freud's metapsychology, the "metaphorical" and "condensational" intricacy of our experiences does not appear at all. He wrote only of id and ego, and held that the "id" has no order and no environmental relations at all.[15]

Beginning from this understanding of instinct and human nature, it is not difficult to understand how religion and the symbolic could offer no realistic hope but instead appear as dangerous illusion. As van Herik observes:

> When Freud detects religion offering the believer a consoling, loving, paternal God, he exposes it as the servant of wish fulfillment. The illusion of the existence and tender loving care of this sort of god is mentally like a feminine attitude towards fathers. . . .
> By emphasizing illusion in its quarrel with reality in *The Future of an Illusion*, Freud built his argument on a theoretical foundation that made its critical result a foregone conclusion: the renunciatory scientific spirit would be better—not salvific, but better.[16]

This worldview of caution and renunciation, though offering important categories for examining the dangerous and debilitating possibilities of relationship and religion, did not satisfy the need to interpret their authentic and reconstructive possibilities. Therefore, my clinical journey continued with a second phase of interaction focusing on Jungian and neo-Jungian interpretation. Indeed, here I found much to delight in and much that nurtured my thinking about human instincts and human nature. Jung's recognition of the need for and function of symbols, the function of the archetypes, the societal illness of the loss of the soul, and the necessity for religion provided a framework of interpretation that allowed for the symbolic and religious dimensions to be understood and positively accessed. As Ann Ulanov and Barry Ulanov have noted

Jung, in contrast [to Freud], recognizes religion as a necessary fact of human experience, providing what we may call true containment for the subterranean, vibrating level of nondirected thinking. He takes the word "religion" to its etymological face value as derived from *religare*, meaning "to bind back," "to bind strongly." But what does religion bind us to? To immediate, primordial, individual experience of the numinous.[17]

As liberating and influential as this contrast was in worldview and orientation, both at the clinical and theoretical levels, a serious problem emerged on both levels as inconsistencies in Jung's theory emerged and as Jung's analysis of the symbolic and the religious began to assume an ontology of its own, leaving little or no room to raise critical questions. Wehr's analysis of this dilemma in Jungian theory has application in the clinical context as well:

On the negative side: the quarrel I have with Jung is with his willingness to consider archetypal phenomena as manifestations of the Divine and with his assertion that we lose something valuable psychologically if we do not see them as such . . . , it is enough here to note that Jung's theory confers religious and ontological status on behaviors, moods, and even uncontrollable vices, which can be explained on other grounds. These grounds do not involve us in categories of the sacred as we try to understand ourselves and others, and to change our behavior, and to become free from stultifying roles and compulsions.[18]

At this point in my search for understanding human nature and human instinct, I had become convinced of the existence of the religious and relational instincts through Jung's influence although I found Jung's thought itself limiting. Freud's influence left its inheritance in the need for a critical and demanding methodology in both theory and clinical work but did not supply a framework for hope.

The third phase of my quest for understanding human instinct came through the theoretical and clinical orientation of feminist metapsychology and methodology. Through exposure to the writings of feminist theorists across disciplines and observing theory in action in different clinical settings, I found a fundamental dimension of hope. This hope for human nature, and for women's development in particular, was based on recognition of the importance of nurture, relationship, spiritual nature, and the need to raise critical questions about theory, therapy, and images of power. This diversified framework exposed the danger of functioning myths about human nature and human illness. Miriam Greenspan's work, for example, exposed three myths about human nature and women's nature in particular that operate in traditional therapy:

Myth 1 tells us that personal reality is essentially determined by unconscious forces within a person's mind.[19]
Myth 2. Closely related to the first, this myth tells us that human emotional pain in our society is a medical problem, that people in such pain

are sick, and that their emotional problems can be cured in the same way that physical problems can: through medical means.[20]

Myth 3. The third myth follows from the first two: if the source of a person's emotional pain is a psychic disease or disorder, then only an expert in diagnosis and treatment is equipped to offer a cure.[21]

The feminist perspective exposed dangerous myths, emphasized the need to raise critical questions, included the social and political as categories for assessment of psychological problems, focused on the importance of understanding power and powerlessness,[22] and urged the use of the full range of emotions as well as the body, spirituality, and ritual in healing and understanding illness.[23] Each influenced my definition and development of the religious and relational instincts. My three-phase and fifteen-year scavenging process has resulted in the naming of the religious and relational instincts as central to Critical Caring.

These central instincts,[24] relational and religious, work in tandem. Together they provide the existential and essential[25] energy dimensions of human existence. The religious instinct is the essential energy dimension. It is the instinct whose energy provides possibilities for connection to the essence of nature and meaning, from its Latin root *religare*, to tie fast, to bind back to the source.[26]

The relational instinct is the existential energy dimension. It is the instinct whose energy provides the enactment of the possibilities of connection, from the Latin root *relatus*, to carry back or refer. Essence and existence are here understood as interdependent. They complement each other so that their energy can be translated into expressions of Critical Caring for self and others. Though these instincts will be expressed differently according to cultural and personal situations, human beings need to acknowledge and understand their importance for psychosocial and psychospiritual health and illness. The religious instinct provides the recognition and awareness of the connections between the human being's internal world and the physical and symbolic world outside. The relational instinct provides the means of expressing these connections.

The religious instinct finds expression in the ability to hope, question, embrace chaos and even doubt, and move toward the future. It is dependent on a degree of trust in the nature and design of the universe and the power that organizes it. In the context of community and culture, the energy of the religious instinct finds expression in the physical and symbolic world. It works toward understanding and experiencing purpose in life and in living. Such purpose is built on the awareness and recognition of connection between God[27] and self, and self and others. The sacred, in the sense of that which makes one recognize and feel hope, is enacted through the religious instinct in the context of experience and awareness. Finally, the religious instinct works in coordination with the mind, soul, and body to cultivate hope, trust, and purpose.

The relational instinct makes interaction possible and finds its fullest expression in acts of love and the giving and receiving of care. The relational instinct is expressed in the physical and symbolic world through different dimensions of meaning-making, always within and through the particular contexts of culture and community. Through the relational instinct the person also experiences connection to the other. In this connection the essential is also expressed through relationship to the self as a whole being whose individual dimensions exist in relationship.

The dimensions of the two instincts can be listed as follows:

Religious instinct
    nurtures the ability to hope, question, embrace chaos and doubt
    trusts in the universe
    understands the symbolic nature of reality
    finds purpose for life and in living
    experiences a sense of connection between God, others, and
        self
    experiences the sacred in the context of living, not removed
        and isolated but infused in the everyday world
    works with reason and the senses to cultivate hope, trust, and
        purpose

Relational instinct
    experiences love
    gives and receives care
    expresses symbolic reality and ritual
    finds ways of making meaning with others
    perceives a connection within the self (body and spirit—all
        parts working together for the whole)
    works with reason and the senses to cultivate love and care

Understanding the religious and relational instincts provides a base for interpreting interaction between people and within a person. For the instincts, the interpersonal and intrapersonal dimensions are parallel. Thus a parallel exists between the microcosm of instincts within each person and the macrocosm of instinctual interaction between persons. As we become conscious of our instinctual nature, it will influence our thinking and imagining. In any given situation the instincts, by their very nature, will operate. Unless they are in some way prevented from operating normally, they will so operate as to propel us toward Critical Caring. If, however, they are blocked in some fashion, their energy will be channeled in a disruptive and damaging manner. This blocking of the central instincts can be understood as contributing significantly to numerous conditions of pathology and to the psychosocial dimensions of illness.

Perhaps the story of Michael, age twenty-one, will give us a working example of how the instincts work and the consequences of their blockage.[28] Michael was orphaned at a young age when his parents died in an automobile accident. His first foster home was with a kind and caring family. Michael has memories of being loved and accepted there. Changes within the family and their relocation led to Michael's second placement at age ten. This new family was, in Michael's words, "hard and abusive to me and their other natural children." This abuse included severe beatings and psychological torture. When the abuse first happened, it took Michael by surprise:

> I had been pretty happy before and I was happy with myself too. I felt I had this core of hope inside that came out sometimes like beams of light to connect with people. But when the beatings started, I first went numb. They continued for a long time. And later I could feel myself fall apart, not outside but inside, and that core of hope began to get smaller, or like got covered over, or something like that. Before I would have really tried to help someone in trouble. Now I felt like I wanted to hurt someone because I was hurting and no one was helping me.

At age thirteen Michael did hurt someone: a younger boy who was unable to defend himself. Michael describes the event:

> So I cornered him and approached him. I was aware that inside now I was really trying to destroy hope. I was pulling and pushing those beams of hope down so they wouldn't interfere with my hate. As I kept punching him, I felt myself dying. I really wanted to die because I—this wasn't living. I had no hope anymore, I knew the core of me was dead. I used to believe in God, but now I felt nothing.

Several years later, Michael again met the young boy he had abused, and this began a healing process for Michael.

> It was like a kind of miracle, I guess. I was in another institution, and he was there also. I was really afraid of him, not because he would hurt me, but because he didn't hate me even after what I did to him. I expected hate from him, and I hated myself enough for both of us. But he was kind to me and told me that if I could learn to forgive me maybe we could spend some time together. This guy, Tony, was some kind of saint maybe. But anyway I took his advice, and we became friends after a while. We are still friends and if I had to I would defend him to the end. He taught me how to heal inside, how to find that core again. It wasn't dead I guess, but I needed his friendship to find it again. And through the friendship I have found my way back to God again. I needed Tony for this too.

In Michael's story we find evidence that the instincts do work naturally with reason. There is no necessary dichotomy between the spiritual and physical dimensions of human life. Perceived dichotomies are, in fact, a product of a different worldview, which will be presented shortly. In fact, healthy human development is dependent on interdependence of all of the dimensions within the self and cooperation between persons. The whole of the self working with the whole of other selves nurtures human development toward maturity. Likewise, other dichotomies such as between genders or among races are not at the core of the instincts. They are learned. The asymmetrical patterns that spring from such dichotomies are not natural to or organized by the instincts.[29]

The religious and relational instincts are at the foundation of Critical Caring. The natural expression of the instincts will lead to Critical Caring. Life is meant to be lived through understanding, encouragement, and facilitation of the instincts, not through working against them.

In order for life to be lived in this manner, the functioning worldview must understand life to be this way. If the functioning worldview is different, the instincts will be understood differently and thereby misunderstood and misdirected. Being instincts, however misunderstood or mislabeled, they will demand expression in some way and through whatever means available, as Michael's story indicates.

For our purposes, the critical question is: Can a hermeneutical foundation create a worldview that understands and nurtures the relational and religious instincts? It will be argued here that a feminist hermeneutic can create such a worldview.[30] Clearly, not all hermeneutical orientations can do this. Certain worldviews—often termed by feminists as androcentric, patriarchal, or oppressive—do not recognize or nurture these instincts but work against them. That is why a feminist hermeneutic is so desperately needed. From a feminist analysis, the dominant worldview has been and continues to be one that denies the nature of the relational and religious instincts, or at best relegates them to a subordinate position.[31] This oppressive worldview, as a consequence of misunderstanding these human instincts, has sorted, labeled, and prioritized human beings by gender, race, belief, sexual expression, and so on. The transition from an oppressive to a feminist worldview is one that necessitates a dramatic shift of focus. Elisabeth Schüssler Fiorenza expresses the force of this shift:

> The shift from an androcentric to a feminist interpretation of the world implies a revolutionary shift in scientific paradigm, a shift with far-reaching ramifications not only for the interpretation of the world but also for its change. Since paradigms determine how scholars see the world and how they conceive of theoretical problems, a shift . . . implies a transformation of the scientific imagination. It demands an intellectual conversion that cannot be logically deduced but is rooted in a change of patriarchal-social relationships.[32]

Schüssler Fiorenza emphasizes the fact that an intellectual conversion is needed, a conversion that cannot emerge out of an oppressive worldview because the basic assumptions are different. A worldview is built from the ground up, from the base of the triangle to the top. This is as true for pastoral psychology as it is for other academic and clinical disciplines. Realizing the need to build a worldview shaped by a feminist hermeneutic of Critical Caring, how then are we to do this?

To do this we need to be clear about two things: first, the philosophy and theology of our Critical Caring worldview, and second, the inheritance of the oppressive worldview that Critical Caring must address. Critical Caring understands human beings as persons whose health, hope, and happiness are based on attention to the relational and religious instincts. Recognition and nurturance of these instincts brings liberation from oppression both within the human being and among persons. Life's vision is one of liberation from oppression. Theological and psychological insights from Schüssler Fiorenza and Sturdivant help to articulate the philosophical and theological truth claims of the Critical Caring worldview.

Theologically, the religious and relational instincts yearn for release in the hope of God's creation. Commitment to this creation marks the "common hermeneutical ground of past, present, and future [which] is not 'sacred history' or 'sacred text' but commitment to the biblical vision of God's new creation."[33] If theology is to be of assistance to the religious instinct, to God's creation, it must understand its role as being "a critical theology of liberation" built from a "historical-biblical hermeneutics of liberation."[34] Existing dichotomies that have fostered rape of the earth and the body must be exposed. Care for the body along with the soul is theology's mission. Wisdom will come, and the instincts will find expression through that which has been neglected, which has been allowed no voice. "Not the soul or the mind or the innermost Self but the body is the image and model."[35]

And finally, as we express our paradigm of liberation and acknowledge the instincts, we must be cautious of being enslaved by the paradigm, seeing it as set once and for all with no room to change. The new paradigm must be approached not as "a timeless archetype but as a historical prototype open to feminist theological transformation."[36]

Psychologically, our understanding of the religious and relational instincts is dependent on our ability to name what is healthful and healing and what is destructive and debilitating. "Every model of human nature contains two explanatory models of human personality. . . . It implies a desired constellation of personality traits . . . , it also holds implications for how psychopathology occurs when things go wrong developmentally."[37] What happens when the models we use are in themselves illness-producing? Sturdivant argues, from a feminist perspective, that psychotherapy must expose its own models and false assumptions about gender that have caused illness and psychological destruction for women.

The core of feminism is simply the insistence that personal autonomy is essential for women. . . . Women should have both the freedom and the responsibility to direct all important areas of their lives: emotional, intellectual, economic, and sexual.[38]

From a feminist perspective, then, assessing psychopathology must include attention to anything that denies that "all roles are open to all people; that every person is entitled to develop his/her potentials to the fullest, unhampered by the restraints of artificially dichotomous sex roles."[39] Psychopathology is never the product of a single person but of a society and culture. The therapeutic context must address the loss of voice and power at all levels. This is done by naming, exposing, and working to correct the imbalance. "Finally, feminism strives to equalize personal power between the sexes."[40]

Critical Caring must be ever alert to what it is working for and working against if the religious and relational instincts are to be nurtured. If Critical Caring is the worldview that understands and nurtures the religious and relational instincts, in contrast, a worldview of oppression works to undermine these instincts. Though we cannot discuss such a worldview at length, its inheritance must be clear. It begins with a fundamentally different approach to understanding human instincts and therefore builds a very different view of human nature. In short, dichotomies and asymmetry dominate oppression's worldview and divide the intrapersonal and the interpersonal worlds in the following way. The person is perceived as a contained unit of warring factions: the instincts (including self-preservation, aggression, domination) work against reason, which itself works against the senses.

This view of the internally warring personality is carried over to an understanding of interpersonal interaction. Persons exist in competition, in a fight for power and domination. Cooperation and relationship are tolerated insofar as they do not interfere with competition and dominating power. Hope, trust, and love are virtually buried in a value system of oppression, and are considered archaic and/or illusory. Life within a worldview of oppression is organized with dualities and asymmetries. Identity is assigned on the basis of certain characteristics or qualifications, and access to power, service, etc., is gained or denied on the basis of this identity. The labeling process is done by those in control. It is difficult or impossible to change one's label. Gender, race, creed, etc., often provide the markers for the labeling process. Power is conceived of from a win-or-lose position. Those with power do not want to lose it and often are themselves terrified of having no power. This creates the need for oppression. Those oppressed usually have few or no options to change. But in such a worldview no genuine peace, hope, trust, or love can survive. Even the "advantaged" are insecure and always fighting to maintain their dominating power. The story of Michael illustrates this tragic reality.

In such a worldview and in such a world there is desperation at every level. The institutions built within or at the margins of such a worldview, whether conscious of the worldview or not, are directly shaped by it. Those institutions will struggle to survive if they threaten the worldview's claims of truth about human nature and values. To question the claims of a worldview of oppression is to question the essential paradigm of dominating power. The worldview of Critical Caring has the means to do so if and only if the threat of a worldview of oppression remains conscious. Critical Caring must be ever vigilant of its need to nurture the religious and relational instincts through the cooperative power of empowerment. Just as Michael encountered a worldview of oppression and struggled to recover his core of hope through friendship and Critical Caring, we also have this opportunity. The field of pastoral psychology can provide a working strategy for gaining this opportunity.

Step 3. Critical Caring in the Field of Pastoral Psychology

Critical Caring and the nurturing of the religious and relational instincts need to be done through many academic fields and in many different clinical contexts. Our concern here is with the field of pastoral psychology and the context of pastoral psychotherapy.

The pastoral field has a unique vantage point from which to understand and nurture the religious and relational instincts and the worldview of Critical Caring. This vantage point is the context of the pastoral. In the pastoral context, which can have many different settings, religious resources are available and faith provides a vital framework for understanding and addressing problems, issues, and concerns. The pastoral context can use the symbolic, sacramental, and liturgical dimensions of faith and community. In order to do this with integrity, the pastoral context needs to reject the theological and philosophical truth claims supporting a worldview of oppression and engage those of Critical Caring. Such engagement will provide access to this worldview for pastoral psychology.

The pastoral context understands the religious and relational instincts as expressed through faith and community. Through the pastoral dimension the instincts are given both literal and symbolic expression. The term "pastoral" refers naturally to its root meaning of "pastor" or "shepherd."[41] This root can be brought from its historical referent to give life in the present if the caring aspect is understood as central. What needs to be left behind is the dimension of the pastoral that fosters an absolute dependency on being the caregiver or the care-receiver. People are not and certainly should not be treated as though they were sheep to be led. This does not lead to Critical Caring as we understand it here. Pastoral caring becomes Critical Caring when the act of caring is understood as necessary for all persons both as givers and receivers.

The word "pastoral" can be understood in another way. Though there is no etymological basis for it, we can visually divide "pastoral" into the words "past" and "oral." Doing this, we now have two words of great relevance for interpreting the pastoral context in light of Critical Caring. "Past" indicates what has come before, the importance of history, memory, and meaning-making. "Oral" indicates the act of speaking and, by extension, naming. It can be understood as a vehicle by which a sorting process takes place to identify and locate thoughts, actions, meanings, things, and persons. If we work with these terms together, we can arrive at a working definition of "pastoral." "Pastoral" means the faith community's ability to articulate its past history, symbols, and rituals of faith; to participate in naming faith's present understandings and use of these; and to work toward interpreting its history, symbols, and rituals for the future. "Pastoral" nurtures active and responsive faith. "Pastoral" becomes a living entity responsible for its heritage and its future through the work of its present.

If we engage this working definition of "pastoral" and combine it with our discussion of Critical Caring, we move toward an approach to pastoral caring in which the pastoral context becomes a responsible one for caring and healing. Pastoral caring can be understood as the faith community's expression of and commitment to Critical Caring. Faith through its words, works, symbols, and rituals embodies its ontology and theology through its ability to care. Through the act of caring, faith finds its primary expression. Pastoral caring is the name of that expression.

In the history of pastoral care, four functions have been identified as central to the act of pastoral caring:[42] healing, guiding, sustaining, and reconciling. These functions have endured over time because they have been interpreted and adjusted as appropriate for faith's expression and ability to care in different time periods and through different communities.

These historical functions can be of great use in pastoral psychotherapy if interpreted through the religious and relational instincts and the hermeneutic of Critical Caring. Theologically and philosophically we must understand human nature as being instinctually relational and religious. The functions have their foundation at the bottom layer of the Triangle of Responsibility (see page 25). The pastoral functions, through the worldview of Critical Caring, are understood as follows: First, the four pastoral functions cooperate with one another to serve and nurture Critical Caring. Though at any given time one of the functions may be emphasized, they are interdependent, and therefore all operate simultaneously. Second, a change in the application of one of the pastoral functions brings a change in the others as well. Third, the functions each operate on the continuum of preventive care through intensive care (the continuum presented in diagram 1; see page 9) and will be of use in whatever combination needed in each pastoral situation. Fourth, each function works toward the energy release of the instincts in their expression of Critical Caring. Through the use of responsible scavenging, each context will determine how the functions will interact and what the functions will need to bring about this release. The pastoral functions are processes and not rigid categories of fixed determination.

Healing is the pastoral function that names the illness or misperception through which uncaring manifests itself and blocks the relational and religious instincts. Healing charts the course toward caring. Illness or misperception always has spiritual as well as psychosocial and physical consequences. The pastoral function of guiding offers the means to and contains the analysis for understanding the nature of this illness or misperception, and outlines the points of danger from the worldview that has led to this. Reconciling serves two purposes. First, it offers a critical, pastoral perspective from which the precise consequences of uncaring can be examined and charted. Second, it offers the possibility for reconnecting that which has been broken or disrupted. The function of sustaining provides the faith and pastoral resources to support the work of critically confronting and responsibly addressing issues, persons, situations, and circumstances from the past and in the present. Each of these functions at times involves difficult, draining, and often emotionally and spiritually painful activity. The pastoral functions provide the critically important movements through which the hermeneutic of Critical Caring brings hope, direction, and new patterns of understanding to human pain and possibility. We can visualize the pastoral functions as concentric levels of activity in the following way (see diagram 3):

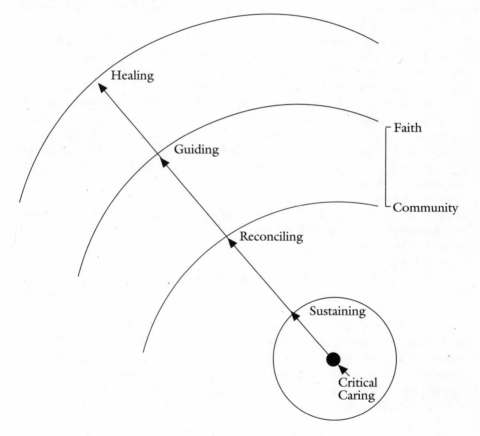

Diagram 3. Pastoral Context Through the Worldview of Critical Caring

Let us examine the hermeneutic of Critical Caring in relation to these pastoral functions by returning to the example of a worldview of oppression. A worldview of oppression claims that "healthy women's development is *dependent* upon the fulfillment of the biological, emotional, and theological need to have a child." In step 1 (see pages 24–27) we examined the theoretical constructs and the philosophical and theological base underlying a worldview of oppression. Now let us examine the life of a human being, Marie, caught in the grip of this oppressive worldview.

Marie was nineteen years old when she was raped by a young man she had begun dating. The man felt he was entitled to sexual favors from his girlfriend. Since Marie had mentioned that she eventually wanted to have a family and children, he reasoned to himself that if Marie became pregnant by the rape he was actually doing her a favor. He saw himself as fulfilling, in some way, the natural course of a woman's development. He did not consider what he did to be rape. He did not feel remorseful about his action. He did not feel responsible when Marie became pregnant.

Marie did feel responsible for her pregnancy and blamed herself for what had happened. She was rejected by members of her family. She was quite alone and desperate. She sought the advice of her minister, who considered her idea of abortion to be against the will of God and the design of life for women. He referred her to a practicing psychotherapist who asked Marie to imagine her pregnancy as a developmental milestone from which she would emerge into womanhood. In desperation she tried to take her own life and almost died. The pregnancy ended in a spontaneous abortion. Marie spent the next five years trying to grieve her loss and to make something of her life. She felt condemned by God, the church, and society.

Here we see the tragic legacy of a worldview in which there is little or no hope or choice for Marie. The cultural attitude, theological perspective, and psychological assumptions leave no room for Critical Caring. There is no room for Marie to care for or respect herself. There is no room for present hope or for the future.

The pastoral functions, if they are to serve Critical Caring, must help Marie find a way to expose, confront, challenge, and destroy this oppressive worldview. They must work at the hermeneutical level to expose the deep illness present at the very center of this hermeneutic of oppression. The function of guiding will expose the theological and psychological roots of oppression, and the legacy of terror present in them. The function of healing will name the illness of hopelessness and prescribe a course of release from this sickness that has blocked the energy of the instincts. Reconciling will chart the depths of pain and the actual consequences at all levels of development for the victims and survivors of this oppression. Through reconciling comes also the empowerment to decide how connections can be made or remade with the past and which connections to make. Sustaining will nurture truth, support grief for what has been lost, and name the betrayal of caring done in the name of theology and psychology. The pastoral functions are not passive, benign activities but powerful forces for the work of Critical Caring, powerful forces through which the relational and religious instincts can be nurtured.

In order for these pastoral functions to be of service in Critical Caring, in the work of pastoral psychology, they must function on the hermeneutical level of investigation and assessment. The hermeneutical level needs to be a part of the clinical work of pastoral psychology. If Marie is to hope again, she must find a pastoral context in which she feels safe enough and sane enough to ask her questions, to find answers to her questions, to name, explore, and challenge the theological and psychological legacies that brought her to the brink of death. This is the challenge to pastoral psychology and for the pastoral functions. This is the hermeneutical challenge of Critical Caring, a challenge that needs to be understood and undertaken in the pastoral clinical context. To meet this challenge we need a conceptual model of human development based on the hermeneutic of Critical Caring. This conceptual model will provide a bridge between where we have been—exploring the hermeneutical analysis of Critical Caring in the foundational level of the Triangle of Responsibility—and where we need to go—a clinical model of Critical Caring that incorporates the levels of theory and technique within the Triangle of Responsibility.

Step 4. Overview Perspective of Human Development

Before a clinical model of Critical Caring can be built, a human development perspective viewed through the hermeneutic of Critical Caring is needed. A perspective of human development provides a bridge between a hermeneutical analysis of the theological and philosophical truth claims of the worldview of Critical Caring and a clinical model of Critical Caring for the context of pastoral psychotherapy. We need an overview perspective on human development as a whole before we are able to enter the particular story of human development that a person or persons bring to the clinical context. Neither a developmental perspective nor a clinical model is meant to be an inflexible universal construction. Rather, they offer starting points for dialogue with concrete situations of human life. The dialogue will then take, shape, and trans-form the model in whatever ways are necessary. Models, even those constructed for the purpose of exposing worldviews of oppression, can themselves become tools for oppression if they are assumed to be universal and applicable in all situations. Thus, from a feminist perspective we build models most responsibly when we consider them to be flexible constructions that need to be refined in and through their encounter with living human stories.[43]

The work of Schüssler Fiorenza in constructing a model for biblical hermeneutics provides an approach to the construction of a working model that is of help for pastoral psychology's task as well. She notes:

Such a model must be a feminist-critical and a historical-concrete model. . . . It should not search for a feminist formalized principle, a universal

perspective, or a historical liberating dynamics but should carefully analyze how the Bible functions concretely in women's struggle for survival.[44]

Her approach to building a model begins with a sense of balance on three levels: between past and present, between analysis and function, and between
abstract and concrete. Her approach to the Bible itself is expressed as follows:
"Rather than reduce its pluriformity and richness to abstract principle or ontological immutable archetype, . . . I suggest the notion of historical prototype
open to its own transformation."[45] In providing a model toward that end,
Schüssler Fiorenza offers five elements:[46]

> Element 1. Suspicion rather than acceptance of biblical authority.
> Function: ". . . is to elaborate as much as possible the patriarchal,
> destructive aspects and oppressive elements in the Bible."[47]

> Element 2. Critical evaluation rather than acceptance.
> Function: ". . . has to articulate criteria and principles for evaluat-
> ing particular texts. . . . Such criteria or principles must be de-
> rived from a systematic exploration of women's experience of
> oppression and liberation."[48]

> Element 3. Interpretation through proclamation.
> Function: ". . . must also assess the contemporary political context
> and psychological function of biblical interpretation and texts."[49]

> Element 4. Remembrance and historical reconstruction.
> Function: "Rather than abandon the memory of our foresisters'
> sufferings, visions, and hopes . . . , such a hermeneutics reclaims
> their sufferings, struggles, and victories through the subversive
> power of the 'remembered' past."[50]

> Element 5. Interpretation through celebration and ritual.
> Function: "Only by reclaiming our religious imagination and our
> ritual powers of naming can women-church dream new dreams
> and see new visions. We do so, . . . in and through a critical
> process of evaluation."[51]

Schüssler Fiorenza's approach and model of biblical hermeneutics can provide a creative resource for pastoral psychology's responsible scavenging process.
Four reasons support this view. First, it presents a means of approach suitable
for a perspective of human development emerging out of a pastoral, feminist
perspective. Second, the five hermeneutical elements (suspicion, evaluation, interpretation through proclamation, remembrance, and interpretation through
ritual) are important elements for a developmental perspective that recognizes
the religious and relational instincts. Third, these elements working in conjunction with the pastoral functions (healing, guiding, sustaining, and reconciling)
can assist the instincts in the developmental process. Fourth, the individual person is always understood to be in the context of community. Diagram 4 presents a perspective of human development in light of Critical Caring.

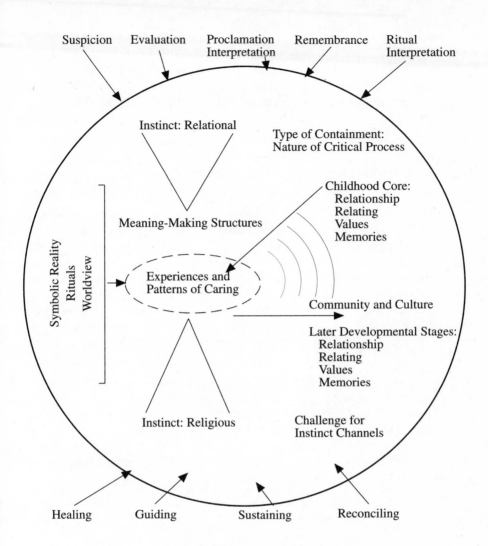

*Diagram 4. Overview Perspective of Human Development
in Light of Critical Caring*

Let us approach the perspective by way of the terms "worldview" (as discussed on page 27) and "symbolic reality," which appear on the left margin of the diagram and which form an overall means of containment for the other parts. The term "symbolic reality," making reference to the work of Arthur Kleinman in medical anthropology, is understood as a bridge between personal and social reality. "Symbolic reality is formed by the individual's acquisition of language and systems of meaning."[52] In order to understand human development, we must understand the worldview operating on that development and the symbol systems at work in it. Therefore, human development may be as functionally varied as are the worldviews we encounter.

In the diagram, situated between "symbolic reality" and "worldview" is "rituals." Rituals serve to connect the meaning-making dimensions of symbolic reality and the expression of those dimensions in the organization of reality through worldview. Clinician and researcher in education and family therapy Janine Roberts offers a definition of ritual from an interdisciplinary perspective:

> Rituals are coevolved symbolic acts that include not only ceremonial aspects of the actual presentation of ritual, but the process of preparing for it as well. It may or may not include words, but does have both open and closed parts which are "held" together by a guiding metaphor.[53]

Roberts's definition stresses the symbolic and social dimensions of ritual, as well as the open (allowing for variation) and closed (established format) parts of ritual expression. These dimensions and parts signal that when persons engage in ritual, there is a possibility for significant change to take place or new insights to be gained. Ritual experiences involve the person within the context of community, of meaning-making. In this kind of enactment, those involved enter into the ritual experience as though preparing for a journey. Through the life cycle there are many ritual experiences. The ones that are the deepest, that link most closely symbolic reality and worldview, are what we shall refer to as religious rituals:

> Religious is here to be understood from the phenomenological as distinguished from the theological perspective. In other words, that which functions as the symbolic meaning-making system is what is meant by religious. The content of the symbol system is therefore analyzed separately from its function as symbol system. Rituals which serve this function of binding and shaping concerns can therefore be termed religious rituals.[54]

In the life cycle religious rituals serve to mediate between memories and frameworks of making-meaning:

> Religious ritual can be understood to be the conduit for meaning and memory's coming together, in the framework of symbolic reality. At whatever stage in the lifecycle a person may be, religious ritual experienced in the present will need to mediate memory and meaning of the past with memory and meaning of the present. Progression through the lifecycle can be understood as the adding of memory and meaning from the past to the present and from the present to the interpretation of the past.[55]

This special function is why it is so devastating for persons when the religious rituals of their past become symbolically empty or become themselves dangerous or illness-producing. When this happens, there is a search for a new ritual that can serve this function. In the therapeutic context, especially in pastoral psychotherapy, there is a unique opportunity for ritual to enter into the therapeutic context for analysis and enactment. Our clinical cases will address ritual, religious ritual, and the consequences of ritual experience as well as strategies for addressing these consequences. For now, however, it is important to keep in mind the significant role rituals play in human development and progression through the life cycle.

It is only with this knowledge that we can proceed to the center of the diagram, the experiences and patterns of caring, understanding that both relate back to worldview, rituals, and symbolic reality. With a perspective of human development understood in light of the Critical Caring process, caring is naturally the pivotal starting place. Experiences and patterns of caring are at the center of human development. Thoughts, behaviors, and values emanate from this center, which is also the container for and interpreter of memories. Structures of relationship and relating are found here as well as the structures of meaning-making. In this respect, experiences and patterns of caring function as the storage center of the past and present, and as the field through which the future is approached consciously or otherwise. Since caring is so foundational to human existence, there are often many experiences and patterns of caring for each person. These experiences and patterns are not individually constructed but are always social, built in the context of community and culture.

These patterns of caring may or may not be in harmony with each other. Conflicting experiences give rise to conflicting patterns of caring and, when analyzed, may reveal patterns of uncaring under the guise of caring. It would be difficult to analyze the meaning-making structures surrounding experiences and patterns of caring without access to the worldview and symbolic reality in which each experience and pattern was created. This permits access to the deep levels of structure, the levels that lie beneath the surface of action and thought.

Moving outward from the center are the stages of development (understood as a process and not as a set of rigid categories) from childhood to adulthood. These stages can be designated in different ways. They can be approached as stages of chronological development by age, by cultural patterns, or as layers of development during which different experiences and patterns of caring have taken place. Transformations or alterations in worldview or symbolic reality can also be charted in this fashion. Understanding stages in this multidimensional way allows the model to be flexible in its use as a tool of analysis for access to a person's development as a whole.

Bounding the stages of development are the central instincts, religious and relational, connected in a circle by arrows indicating movement. These are so situated in the diagram for two reasons. First, they are instincts, forces of energy and movement that are never fully contained in points of time or location but are expressed in points of time and location. However, this expression is mediated through worldview, symbolic reality, community, and culture. Therefore the instincts are placed as the energy field surrounding the person's development.

In the outermost part of the diagram can be found the five hermeneutical functions and the four pastoral functions. The hermeneutical functions are used to explore and assess the patterns of caring through the life cycle. The pastoral functions explore and assess the experiences of caring. Together they work to link experience with pattern and to show the consequences to the Critical Caring process at any particular point in time, as well as the results over time. More will be said on the clinical interaction between the five hermeneutical functions—suspicion, evaluation, proclamation interpretation, remembrance, and ritual interpretation—and the four pastoral functions—healing, guiding, sustaining, and reconciling—in the next chapter, but let us return to the story of Marie to illustrate the use of these hermeneutic and pastoral functions in the model of development.

We encounter Marie when she is twenty-four, living on her own in another part of the city from which the experience at nineteen happened. Marie is still feeling unsettled and wondering why she cannot, in her words, "shake myself free of that time, and stop feeling so responsible for everything. It's like my life on the outside has changed but inside I am almost frozen in that time."

How can Marie be assisted to shake herself free? The answer to this question must come from Marie, but it is a question that is centered at the hermeneutical level. Somehow, Marie needs to develop a perspective in the present that can allow her to look at that part of her past and name it for what it was. The functions can help with this process in two ways. First, they can be used to establish a safe present perspective. If Marie can name and gain access to the patterns in her life that now nurture her, she can begin to articulate a perspective through which she can feel more secure. Second, the work of the hermeneutical functions in creating a present perspective may eventually help Marie to explore the patterns and truth claims of her past, evaluate them, raise questions of suspicion about these patterns, remember incidents without getting lost in the memory, interpret the past through proclaiming and naming it in a new way, and interpret through ritual, symbol, and action the containment of her past and the way to her future. In short, the hermeneutical functions can help Marie to decode the hermeneutical foundation upon which past patterns were constructed. If this can be accomplished, Marie may be able to remember and examine past experiences strengthened by her hermeneutical awareness and the freedom it offers.

While Marie works with the hermeneutical task of naming nurturing patterns in her present, the pastoral functions can support her. The very act of naming one's hermeneutical perspective is a labor of no small magnitude. The functions of healing, guiding, sustaining, and reconciling can offer Marie strength and direction in this process. And as she moves toward naming the patterns and truth claims of her past, the pastoral functions help Marie to experience present stability and direction. If Marie is able to uncover and name the damaging patterns of her past and keep herself grounded in the present, she can move to remember and examine the actual experiences of these patterns that have caused her pain and anguish. The pastoral functions, using all available pastoral resources, can assist Marie to name and grieve for the experiences of uncaring and harm that she experienced. The naming and grieving can help Marie to put these experiences in perspective, not to forget them but to have present control over them. Grieving and naming can lead to action, literal and/or symbolic, moving from the present to address the past. And through the grieving, naming, and acting expressed through word, deed, and ritual, Marie may find release from her unsettledness in order to experience caring toward herself in the present and future.

The hermeneutical functions and the pastoral functions can thereby assist not only with analysis and assessment of past patterns of uncaring and development but also with the creation of new patterns and experiences of caring, new stages of development, and opportunities for Critical Caring. These functions can assist in developing the art of responsible scavenging in examining and salvaging from the past, in decision-making in the present, and in identifying resources of Critical Caring for the future.

CHAPTER 3

A Clinical Model of Critical Caring for Pastoral Psychotherapy

In chapter 1 we examined the concept of Critical Caring and the nature of the umbrella field of pastoral psychology with special reference to its subfield of pastoral psychotherapy. In chapter 2 we moved from the concept of Critical Caring to an exploration of the feminist hermeneutic of Critical Caring for pastoral psychology and ended with an overview perspective of human development. This perspective can be conceived as a bridge between a hermeneutical analysis of Critical Caring and a clinical model of Critical Caring for pastoral psychotherapy. In this chapter we will journey over this bridge as we build a clinical model of Critical Caring.

Before we can build a clinical model, we need to understand its nature and relationship to the Triangle of Responsibility (see diagram 2 on page 25). We must first ask the question: How does a clinical model for pastoral psychotherapy relate to the hermeneutical work of Critical Caring? The answer of relationship encompasses two levels: the technical and the substantial. At the technical level, with reference to the Triangle of Responsibility, a clinical model represents the theory and technique sections of the triangle. Diagram 5 can help us visualize this relationship.

The bottom level of the triangle contains the worldview and truth claims of the feminist hermeneutic of Critical Caring. The level just above is that of theory. This is the theoretical orientation by which the hermeneutic of Critical Caring is translated into a working clinical model. The perspective of human development serves as a bridge between these levels. And finally, the level of

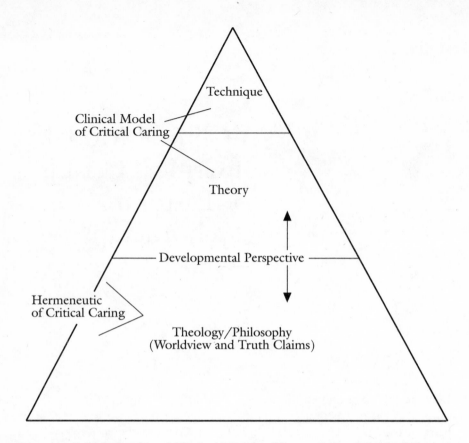

Diagram 5. Relationship of Clinical Model to Hermeneutic of Critical Caring

technique incorporates the hermeneutical perspective and theoretical orientation of Critical Caring for interaction in the clinical context.

This has been a description of the technical link between the hermeneutic of Critical Caring and a clinical model of Critical Caring. The technical link is built on a substantial link, a link of substance between the hermeneutic, the developmental perspective, and that which takes place in the clinical context. If life, at its hermeneutical foundation, is understood as the challenge to care critically, and the perspective of human development is constructed with reference to Critical Caring, then the theory of the therapeutic and its clinical context need to be part of Critical Caring as well. This is the link of substance between the levels of the Triangle of Responsibility. This link indicates that the therapeutic experience and the clinical context are opportunities through which Critical Caring can take place.

The clinical model of Critical Caring has evolved over time and through exploration of the needs, insights, critical questions, and struggles of people engaged in the therapeutic process of Critical Caring in pastoral psychotherapy. After a brief look at the model, we will explore it more extensively by addressing the following questions. First, what is the nature of pastoral psy-chotherapy in light of Critical Caring? Second, how do the pastoral functions and the hermeneutical functions work in the clinical context model of Critical Caring? Third, what is the therapeutic task for pastoral psychotherapy as expressed in the clinical model of Critical Caring?

The clinical model of Critical Caring (diagram 6) consists of six episodes in the clinical process. These episodes have at their center the Triangle of Responsibility as an ongoing point of reference and stability, and the perspec-tive of development through Critical Caring as the organizing point for

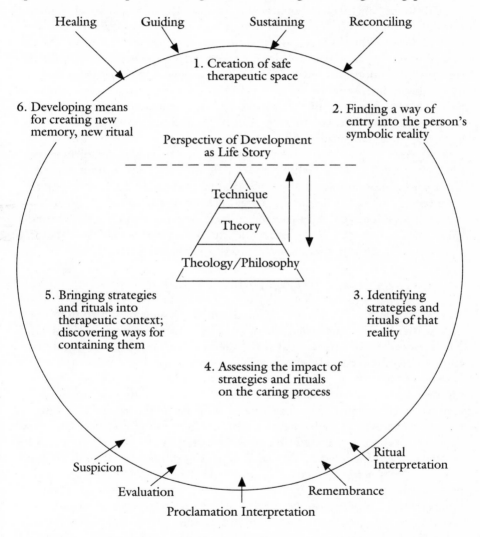

Diagram 6. Clinical Model of Critical Caring for Pastoral Psychotherapy

the experiences and patterns of the life story of the person or persons involved in the therapeutic process. The pastoral and the hermeneutical functions encircle the six episodes of the clinical process as they provide a means to access and assess the experiences and patterns of the past and present as the therapeutic episodes move toward a future in which Critical Caring can find new expression.

Question 1: What Is the Nature of Pastoral Psychotherapy in Light of Critical Caring?

Building on the hermeneutical orientation of pastoral psychotherapy through Critical Caring, we will examine the nature of pastoral psychotherapy in light of Critical Caring in terms of three dimensions. The first is the nature of the therapeutic relationship; the second is the space and context for the therapeutic relationship; and the third is the process of therapeutic movement. These three dimensions are understood to exist in and through the context of faith. Though there are different contexts of the therapeutic, when we are dealing with the pastoral context in any of its different forms, we begin with the assumption that faith itself be understood as a context for expression of the central instincts. In the pastoral framework it is never only an individual person's religious system and faith symbols that are important to understand but also their location in a community of meaning-making. It is vital that one also comprehend the way beliefs and theological assumptions influence faith and action. If a person has chosen a pastoral context, as is the case with the four individuals whose pastoral psychotherapeutic experiences we will discuss in the next chapters, then the adjective "pastoral" needs to be taken seriously.

Nature of the Pastoral Therapeutic Relationship

When faith is considered an important dimension of the context itself, then particular religious beliefs, theological assumptions, religious rituals, and symbols need to be able to find their way into the therapeutic context. This entrance needs to include examination, analysis, and assessment. Yet in the pastoral context there needs also to be a way to move beyond assessment to the next level, the nurture and movement of faith for the individual in the context of community. The four functions of pastoral care and the pastoral process are located in the context of a faith community. In whatever imaginative and appropriate ways possible, this faith-community context needs to be recognized and included in Critical Caring. Knowledge of the faith community is important for understanding not only the context of faith to which a person belongs or has belonged but also the impact of that context on the Critical Caring process, on the ways in which the religious and relational instincts have been nurtured or impeded in that context.

The faith community provides a contextual metaphor for the pastoral therapeutic relationship. This relationship, though not a faith community itself or a replacement for such, can be understood as an experiencing of community through faith for the purpose of Critical Caring empowerment. In this experience of community, it is important that the pastoral therapeutic relationship be understood as a working relationship built on a common goal: to empower the Critical Caring process. This pastoral relationship works best when both therapist and client understand that they are working as partners. The therapist is a partner and not a distant pastoral expert, not the supreme guide but a resource person for the work that is to be done. When understood as a working partnership, as an experience of community, there is a deliberate and existential recognition of the presence and involvement of faith, God, and others as the therapeutic process warrants. This partnership understands and appreciates God's energy within the context of the therapeutic relationship. If the faith context is taken seriously, then the primary symbols of that faith need to enter into the dynamics of the relationship itself. Though they may take a number of forms, as our exploration of the model and the cases will indicate, nevertheless an overarching assumption should be that the person's primary symbols and way of understanding faith will find expression and enter into the therapeutic process.

As God's presence is experienced and the primary symbols of faith are represented, other persons may enter into the therapeutic process by invitation. The therapeutic experience of community, between therapist and client, needs to assess those communities of accountability and responsibility in which a person is involved. Involvement of different members of these communities in the therapeutic process may be important at times. In other words, the therapeutic relationship should be one that allows for responsible invitation and experimentation with the communities of faith or the communities of meaning-making to which the individual person is or has been accountable, or to which she or he is moving in terms of further work and development. One might say that the pastoral therapeutic relationship is an experience of a temporary community of partnership based on the hope of empowerment. Through this community of partnership, this facilitating experience, the person may be able to work toward Critical Caring partnerships within the communities of meaning-making in which she/he is involved.

The image of the pastoral therapeutic relationship as a temporary faith community of partnership has emerged in light of the nature of this very particular kind of relationship. Though a temporary relationship, it can be very intense as well. In this temporary, intense period, a partnership of trust and cooperation needs to be formed so that energy can be released and directed toward undertaking the challenges that emerge in the therapeutic process. When working in this way, the members of this therapeutic partnership exist and function as a microcosmic faith community, linked to the language, symbols, stories, and rituals of the larger faith community. Understanding the therapeutic relationship in this way permits conscious access to the resources of a faith community. In situations where a person is no longer involved with a larger faith community, or where problems are emerging from such involvement, the therapeutic relationship can serve as an opportunity for exploring the nature and meaning of a faith community. In certain situations, the person may need to free herself or himself from a community whose expression of faith is not one of empowerment but oppression, and the therapeutic relationship understood as a temporary faith community of partnership can help with this difficult process and the challenges posed by the search for a new faith community.

Space and Context of Pastoral Psychotherapy

The second dimension for pastoral psychotherapy in light of Critical Caring is the space and context of pastoral psychotherapy for the therapeutic relationship. The point here is not so much to place emphasis on a particular space, a particular room, although the pattern is generally that one would choose a space and stay with it. The point here is that the room, the meeting place, the therapeutic context, itself becomes an important space and context both physically and symbolically for the therapeutic relationship. When one is engaged in the process of pastoral psychotherapy within the larger context of faith, one has embarked intentionally on a journey of exploration.

Preparation for this journey needs to anticipate interaction between past memory and present function. Such interaction is challenging, usually exhausting, and often difficult. This interaction between past memory and meaning-making and present meaning-making and strategizing is necessary for the therapeutic process. If this is the process and focus, if these are the kind of discoveries that can be expected, then the therapeutic space and context need to be transformed into a safe and responsible place in which exploration of this type of material is possible. Therefore, one of the greatest challenges to be dealt with at the beginning of the pastoral therapeutic relationship is the literal and symbolic tending to space and context.

If the person coming for therapy does not feel that it is a safe space, a space claimed in and through therapeutic partnership, then it will be difficult, dangerous, or impossible for that person to feel that she or he is able to undertake the necessary journey. Through the therapeutic partnership, trust is built and through this trust the therapeutic space is made safe. Intentional discussions about the therapeutic space and context, inviting the client to talk about her or his concerns about space and context, provide in themselves ways to build a safe and responsible therapeutic relationship. The tangible, physical, actual world of the therapeutic space becomes a reflection of the therapeutic partnership, the experience of community built from and working toward Critical Caring.

Therapeutic Movement

The third dimension of pastoral psychotherapy to be explored in light of Critical Caring is the process of therapeutic movement. The therapeutic process happens for both client and therapist. In my experience, the most accurate way of describing the therapeutic process is as a search for ways to build perspectives and devise strategies for living in a caring and critical way. Having said that, it is important to understand that no one person can have the answer for another. The building of perspective and devising of strategy are unique for each individual and will involve the art of responsible scavenging from all appropriate communities of meaning-making. The therapeutic process can be understood as a context for encouraging, inviting, and nurturing persons to discover the ways in which they need to do their own responsible scavenging. The therapeutic process is best understood as cyclical and not linear, although it takes place over time. Time can be measured in linear terms. However, it is better understood as a cyclical process of many beginnings, many middles, and many endings. Time and movement in this process are woven together to become a therapeutic tapestry. Movement takes place in and out of a fascinating pattern of design whereby strands, woven and rewoven, evolve into very complicated patterns. If the therapeutic process works, it will involve the constant weaving and interweaving of strands of a person's life with other lives, symbols, and ways of making-meaning.

2. How Do the Pastoral Functions and the Hermeneutical Functions Work in Relation to the Model?

Moving to our second question concerning the work of the pastoral and the hermeneutical functions, we need first of all to have a clinical definition of the individual functions themselves. The pastoral function of healing provides safe access, by way of faith, from the pain of the past to the hope of the present. This is dependent on the person being able to understand the importance of caring for herself or himself as part of what healing means. The pastoral function of guiding works with the critical ability of an individual to investigate situations and make responsible decisions. Guiding involves trusting in oneself through relationship with God and with others. The third function, sustaining, is the ability to identify values and patterns of importance to the work of the religious and relational instincts as one moves through both the more stable and the more transitory dimensions of life. Sustaining needs to be done and encouraged by the self in relationship.

And finally, reconciling is the ability to assess the various myths and symbols of the past and present in order to decide which symbols and myths will interpret faith and hold hope for the future. Reconciling too depends on an individual being able to assess for herself or himself, working with the tools of Critical Caring. Looking at these pastoral functions from a pastoral feminist perspective, it is important to note that we emphasize the work the self must do. This is not done outside relationship but inside relationship. Emphasis is on the work a person must do *for* herself or himself, not *by* herself or himself.

The five hermeneutical functions—suspicion, evaluation, interpretation through proclamation, remembrance, and interpretation through ritual—can be of service in the clinical work of Critical Caring as well. These functions are concerned with how we understand and interpret reality, and how we name its dimensions. These hermeneutical concerns are vital in the clinical context as persons work to gain access to how they make meaning and how their reality is formed. Suspicion is the ability to step back from a situation and assess the positive and negative dimensions, the myths and symbols at work. Suspicion also involves developing the ability to see a situation as multilevel and complicated. It encourages the ability to decipher and distinguish. Remembrance is the ability to separate the present perspective from past perspectives. Remembering is best done when one is able to know that memories brought to consciousness are not current dimensions of life. This is possible only if one is able to understand perspective and distinguish between different vantage points. This involves being able to stay in the present in order to examine the past without becoming lost in it or overpowered by it. Interpretation through proclamation is the conscious ability to sort, name, and declare the symbols and myths of the present that will lead to hope and health. Evaluation is the ability to test, refine, and assess the circumstances of the present so that movement can take place toward hope and health for the future. Finally, interpretation through ritual is the whole person's expression of reality both physically and symbolically. Responsible ritual expression involves the creation of a therapeutic context that is experienced as safe and able to contain the energy released through the ritual process.

These nine functions, the four pastoral and the five hermeneutical, become especially energy giving as they emerge in the real-life situations brought to the pastoral psychotherapeutic context. The energy exchange comes as one begins to understand the pain and confusion in the symbols of the past and present that come to consciousness in the present. A visible pattern of energy release is followed by energy strengthening in the delicate and often difficult process of naming those myths, symbols, experiences, and patterns of the past that have led to negative and destructive patterns. Only when the negative patterns have been named, can the positive patterns be put in perspective and their energy engaged. The pastoral context offers, or should be able to offer, not only the context for discussing and analyzing those negative and positive religious myths and symbols but more importantly a context for engaging these myths and symbols and moving toward reconstruction through Critical Caring.

Addressing myths, symbols, experiences, and patterns in the pastoral therapeutic context involves the four pastoral and five hermeneutical functions' assessing and interacting with past and present religious rituals and the actual expressions of myths and symbols. Assessing and interaction include but also go beyond discussion and analysis to the reconstructive work of bringing ritual and symbol directly into the therapeutic process. Other therapeutic contexts may also choose to involve ritual, but the pastoral context cannot afford not to engage it. The pastoral context is able to engage ritual, myth, and symbol through faith and community accountability. No other therapeutic context has this particular vantage point and therefore this unique means for reconstruction.

In the pastoral clinical model of Critical Caring, the pastoral and hermeneutical functions appear at the top and bottom. They form an outer circle representing an active cycle surrounding the therapeutic process. The pastoral and hermeneutical functions offer their own energy for the therapeutic process. The functions are used in different ways in the therapeutic process. They are sometimes brought directly into the process itself, being used by persons to assess their own situation and direction. At other times a client will work with one or another as appropriate. At all times the pastoral psychotherapist can make use of them as assessment and analysis resources for understanding the process itself, charting movement, and identifying areas for clarification.

At different points in the therapeutic process it is useful to understand how these two sets of functions may come together to work in tandem. For instance, we can imagine the pastoral function of sustaining working in conjunction with the hermeneutical function of suspicion forming the hybrid function of sustaining suspicion. Sustaining suspicion has proven to be an important hybrid function in many of the cases that I have worked with because the sustaining of suspicion, the sustaining of the healthy, responsible development of critical questions is essential for the ability to ask further questions and work toward decision making. Likewise, the functions can be reversed to give us suspicious sustaining whereby a past or present pattern of sustaining, a pattern assumed to be nurturing, comes under investigation for its ability to aid Critical Caring.

Another hybrid function is reconciling remembrance. This can be understood as coming to terms with the past and intentionally setting a perspective, especially for those who have a difficult time keeping the past in the past and the patterns of the past from clouding the movement of the present. Remembering reconciling involves intentional recall of a situation in which reconciling happened in order to offer hope in the middle of a difficult and felt-to-be-hopeless situation.

Healing proclamation uses the activity of healing toward the ability and encouragement of the sorting and naming process. Proclaiming healing is often used in a preventive way to encourage strength and perseverance during a critical therapeutic interval. Guiding evaluation brings together the ability of the self to trust in self through relationship and to name the categories and strategies for assessment. The combination of functions is almost limitless as they work in pairs and in aggregates to aid the therapeutic process.

The functions working on their own or in conjunction with one another can be understood as spiritual energy resources that help to bind the therapeutic relationship and the work that is to be done there. I have found it very helpful as part of the empowering process and as an encouragement for Critical Caring to talk about the different functions with persons in the therapeutic context. At times talking about these functions provides a way for a person to understand not only particular symbols, myths, patterns, and experiences but, more importantly, how they work in terms of the way people approach their faith and life. Often, after being introduced to these functions, clients will refer to them and develop their own means for using them in the therapeutic process (see especially chapter 7 for an explicit example of this).

Having the pastoral functions and the hermeneutical functions working conjointly at the boundary of the therapeutic process allows for the therapeutic process itself to be understood in terms of a larger context of faith and community. These different functions, forming the working boundary of the model, help to locate the pastoral therapeutic context's movement and activity connected to the larger spiritual community, connected to the faith community's expression of these functions as the work of the religious and relational instincts.

Seeing a diagram of the clinical model of Critical Caring and talking about the pastoral and hermeneutic functions can become empowering. Sometimes a person will use the model as a vantage point from which to think about the functions and goals she or he wants to accomplish in therapy. Though naturally not everyone will choose actively to use the model, it has proven to be helpful both for providing a perspective for naming the therapeutic process and as a strategy for going forward. In other words, it helps the person to keep her or his work on track, which is an important dimension of the empowerment process. The presence of the functions at the perimeter of the clinical model also reminds the therapist to be ever mindful of her or his own myths, symbols, experiences, and patterns that need to be assessed so that they do not interfere with the therapeutic process. The functions may assist the pastoral psychotherapist with this self-assessment process.

The self-assessment process for the pastoral psychotherapist is vitally important for the therapeutic relationship. Insights gained through this process can, where and when appropriate, be brought into the therapeutic context. Often, for persons struggling with a challenging situation or confronting a difficult choice, it is helpful to know that the pastoral psychotherapist has struggled as well. The psychotherapist's sharing of stories in the clinical context can offer evidence that people can find their way through difficulties and learn to question things in a positively critical and caring way. Sharing such stories is not to suggest solutions or to recommend strategies but rather to empower the other to do her or his own responsible scavenging in order to safely experiment with alternatives and strategies. This kind of responsible sharing is one dimension of the therapeutic partnership that emphasizes the co-humanity of the partners and thereby the co-possibilities of the therapeutic context.

3. What Is the Work of Pastoral Psychotherapy as Expressed in the Clinical Model of Critical Caring?

Our third question leads us to the nature of and movement through the model itself. The model has emerged out of clinical experience. It has been refined through communication and consultation not only with clinical and academic colleagues but also with those special colleagues who have been my partners in the therapeutic context.

The model expresses the evolutionary nature of therapeutic movement in and toward Critical Caring. Movement through the model involves six episodes. It is important to understand the episodes as overall patterns of movement in contrast to carefully delineated, linear, progressive steps.

Movement happens through these episodes over the course of the therapeutic process. It is also important to remember that the presentation of case material through this six-episode cycle is done from the therapist's perspective at the completion of the cycle. This perspective is shaped from a distance, when the therapeutic cycle is complete.

The six episodes are understood as evolving in their complexity and intensity. One person in the therapeutic process described it "as a different color being added at each of the episodes so that by the time you get to the final episode you have a rich and varied pattern that is composed of each of the episodes prior to it." The image of a rich, multicolored pattern as a metaphor for the episodes is helpful because at different points it is necessary to peel back the "colors," to remember what has happened in prior episodes. People go through the six-episode cycle at different rates and with different rhythms. For instance, the material that surfaces concerning past traumatic events will often take longer to work its way through the cycle than issues emerging from the present, which have a different perspective and for which resources can be channeled in a different way. It is not only possible but probable that one may be in the later episodes of the cycle but still need to return to the work of prior episodes to explore certain issues. One moves as one needs to through the cycle. There is no wrong way to move, and people need to be encouraged to move in a way that will empower them in the process. Each episode of the cycle incorporates its own encouragement of responsible scavenging for all partners involved.

Episode 1. Creation of Safe Therapeutic Space

The first episode of the cycle involves the creation of a safe therapeutic space. There are no time limits on the length of time one stays in an episode. Even after one moves from this episode there will be times of return to the resources found here as difficult issues emerge. The creation of safe therapeutic space is always a multilevel process involving physical, spiritual, symbolic, and personal dimensions. The process is also always interpersonal. This is a reminder that the therapeutic relationship is a partnership. The more tangibly a person can claim the therapeutic space and actively work to engage it as a safe space, one in which trustworthy things can happen, the more likely it is that the person will be able to trust the space and therefore what happens within it. The therapist needs to bring respect and encouragement for the development of the space as safe space but should be prepared for the possibility of resistance.

If a person has experienced her or his space—personal, symbolic, physical, and/or spiritual—as having been violated once or many times, then the encouragement to create a safe therapeutic space should also be accompanied by the encouragement to be suspicious about the very creation of such a space. Some of the most useful work I have participated in concerning the creation of safe therapeutic space has been when the person has allowed herself or himself to engage the function of suspicion. When suspicions can be raised about the myths of creating a safe space, there may follow an understanding and respect for what has come before in a person's life. The task of building a safe space may be and indeed may need to be very difficult for such a person. Yet, understanding and trusting the resistance will often allow a hope for safety and trust to evolve through the therapeutic relationship.

Episode 2. Entry Into Symbolic Reality

Once a degree of safety and trust in the space, in the process, and in the relationship has been established, a person can release energy to begin exploring present meaning-making patterns. The work of assisting someone in the building of a perspective, the ability to ask critical questions and sort through issues, involves movement to the second episode: finding a way of entry into a person's symbolic reality. This stage is usually one that the person anticipates to be fairly straightforward and sometimes it is. More often, however, this stage is complicated. The complication is that rather than a single symbolic reality in the person's life there are different symbol systems and symbolic realities at work. Sorting through them is a very time-consuming and complex process. Finding a way of entry into a person's symbolic reality involves naming and distinguishing between realities of the present and past. Creating a perspective of symbolic reality in the present allows for greater distance to be given to the naming of past symbolic realities.

Wherever possible, naming and discussing symbolic realities should be accompanied by a person's bringing symbols of these realities into the therapeutic context as they feel comfortable doing so. The presence of symbols often helps the perspective-building process by having physical objects at hand that can be touched and moved. The presence of symbols helps to involve all of the person in the therapeutic process and, by extension, the communities of meaning-making.

Episode 3. Identifying Central Strategies
and Rituals of Symbolic Reality

Finding ways of entry into a person's symbolic reality leads to the third stage of the cycle: the identifying of central strategies and rituals of that reality. Movement from episode two to three is often unnoticed but significant. This movement indicates the person's transition from trusting the naming of the symbolic reality to the building of a perspective in the present that will allow for a process of sorting through that reality. Through identifying central strategies and rituals of that reality, the values of that reality or realities will surface.

The more realities in number and complexity, the slower and sometimes more ponderous the process of identifying strategies and rituals becomes. This stage is critically important and is often accompanied by exhaustion. Naming the strategies and rituals in past and present symbolic realities necessitates a coming to terms with the nature and consequences of those realities.

Episode 4. Assessing the Impact of Strategies and Rituals on the Caring Process

Coming to terms with the nature of past and present symbolic realities brings us to the fourth episode: assessing the impact of strategies and rituals on the caring process. As one moves through episodes two, three, and four, one moves more deeply into the naming and assessing process. However, assessing the nature of symbolic reality is less intense than assessment of the impact of the strategies and rituals of symbolic reality on the caring process. Therefore, entering episode four can be done most responsibly when the person is able to understand the importance of building perspective and maintaining critical distance.

If a person is involved with many symbolic realities and different symbol systems, sometimes she or he can explore the impact of one system but not another. The person has learned how to exist in one system but not how to deal with the impact of the others. Although this episode often appears as a very logical one, progression through this episode can sometimes be agonizing for a person. Anticipation and preparation for this need to be part of the therapeutic process.

Episode 5. Bringing Strategies and Rituals Into the Therapeutic Process and Discovering Ways for Containing

When a person is able to gain the perspective that allows for naming, identifying, and assessing the impact of strategies and rituals on past and present patterns of caring, only then is the person able to bring these often dangerous or unsettling strategies and rituals into the therapeutic context. This is not to say that there will be no rituals or strategies involved before this in the therapeutic process. In fact, in the very first episode, the creation of a safe therapeutic space, bringing in symbols, and performing rituals may be very useful. Rituals of protection or enlightenment are to be encouraged from the beginning of the therapeutic process.

But the art of the therapeutic also involves the science of timing. To therapeutically enact rituals of abuse or painful unprocessed symbols before a safe therapeutic space is established or before a safe perspective has been built is potentially very destructive. Work needs to be done in the therapeutic process to uncover ways or to discover ways for containing these rituals and symbols. To bring to consciousness without preparation is to engage in a critically irresponsible activity. Once the person has developed a perspective, can maintain a reasonable boundary, and has an active symbolic and ritual resource network, then the strategies and rituals that need containment can be brought most safely into the therapeutic context.

Episode 6. Developing Means for Creating New Memory, New Ritual

Movement from the fifth to the sixth episode involves the intentional use of the therapeutic context to design or redesign, create or recreate rituals, strategies, and memories. Over time the therapeutic experience itself becomes a new memory resource. Therefore, if new rituals and strategies can be developed and tested in the therapeutic context, then a new memory for containing rituals and strategies of the past can be made. A new ritual accompanies rather than replaces a ritual of the past. Ritual works to contain ritual as memory works to contain memory. There is not destruction but containment of past ritual, strategy, or memory.

The techniques used in the therapeutic process in general and in the sixth episode in particular vary significantly in terms of the needs of the particular person, the nature of the person, and the ways in which the person makes meaning. Understanding and incorporating techniques such as story, dance, ritual, prayer, etc., as part of the therapeutic process can help to reach the resources of the whole person. Frequently, using one or more of these techniques in the creation of a ritual or special ceremony will release memory or energy for further work.

Three Final Notes About the Clinical Model of Critical Caring

1. A person may go through the episodes of the cycle for one issue, test it, and then come back to the beginning of the cycle, or at least to its resources to work with another issue. However, moving through the cycle for a second or third issue is itself now a known process. Momentum has been gained. It is wisest not to have set expectations about how someone will go through the cycle. It is helpful to encourage freedom of movement so that moving through the cycle does not itself become a psychological burden.

2. The functional nature of the cycle in each episode is a movement of trust for the person in terms of becoming familiar with the myths, rituals, and strategies that have influenced their meaning-making process. Influence can be helpful or harmful, but remaining ignorant of what has been and is influential is more harmful. The process of becoming familiar with self is part of the therapeutic process, and it is guided by the relational and religious instincts. These help the person in her or his art of responsible scavenging of the past, in the present, and for the future.

3. The process of sorting through symbolic realities is never an easy one. It is especially challenging because so often both the positive reconstructive work and the negative destructive work of these realities is connected to dimensions of religious belief, images of God, images of self, and value systems whose roots are connected to faith images and theological belief systems. Perhaps one of the most significant dimensions of the building and nurturing of a safe therapeutic space and safe therapeutic relationship is the pastoral psy-

chotherapist's encouragement to the person to honestly address the negative dimensions of her or his religious beliefs or theological inheritance without feeling that such honesty is against the will of God or is a spiritual offense.

In the process of therapeutic partnership, the pastoral therapist is constantly challenged to critically care. With each new person, the episodes come to life and go through a new refining process. For the pastoral therapist the legacy of memories of persons moving toward Critical Caring can be powerful and sustaining.

Selection of Clinical Cases

The next four chapters focus on different applications of the clinical model of Critical Caring. The cases have been selected for several reasons. First, they represent persons, female persons, at different points in the life cycle, in different situations, and facing different needs. Second, in each case religious belief and theological orientation present a problematic situation for spiritual health and psychosocial development. Third, in each case the problematic belief and theological orientation need to be recognized, explored, and responsibly challenged in and through the pastoral therapeutic context if healing is to take place. Fourth, these cases, each in a different way, have proven to be a pastoral and clinical challenge to me as pastoral psychotherapist. Through them I have wrestled with my own symbolic reality and my therapeutic understanding of the nature and role of pastoral psychotherapy. They have engaged me in the Critical Caring process and for that, and to my therapeutic partners represented here, I will be forever appreciative. Fifth and finally, each of the persons on whom the representations are built has given her permission for her story to be told and her journey through the episodes to be shared. Each has chosen the code names used in the case presentation.

One final note: The cases are presented through a method whereby they evolve as a total, therapeutic story with description, analysis, and assessment as part of a unified presentation. I am thankful to my clinical colleagues for the recommendation of this method for case presentation as I think it allows for an accurate and responsible way to tell a thorough clinical story. The case presentations focus on the nature and use of the clinical model of Critical Caring and are structured according to the model's six-episode format.

PART 2

CHAPTER 4

The Case
of Heather:
Images for Silence;
Images for Hope

I. Overview and Background

In this case the person involved in pastoral psychotherapy is a child, Heather, age six. Heather has a twin brother, Henry. Her parents, Susan and David, aged thirty-one and thirty-six respectively, come from a small city in the middle of the United States. Her parents moved to a larger city in the Midwest when Heather and Henry turned three. The family background is German and English. Susan is currently a homemaker working part-time giving music lessons. She has a college degree in music. David is an engineer. Susan and David have been married eight years. There are no other children in the family.

Susan and David have been members of a conservative Christian church for the past three years. The teachings of this church include a strong theological belief in different gender roles and divinely ordered gender purposes. Heather and Henry have been in the church preschool program.

To create an accurate point of entry into Heather's situation, the relating of a church school incident is necessary. Heather and Henry participate in the same church school class, though there are two parallel kindergarten classes. In one of their lessons, the teacher, Mrs. Green, asked them to draw a picture of God. God had been described to the children in male terms as "Father and Provider" through scripture and other religious materials. Henry drew a picture of God with a face similar to his father's, including a beard. Heather drew a picture of God with two faces, one male and the other female.

When the teacher saw Heather's drawing, her response was surprise and dismay. Heather remembers the teacher saying, "No, that's not what God looks like. God the Father is male. God doesn't have two faces." Henry remembers the look on the teacher's face: "She had a mean look on her face, like Heather had done something bad." Heather felt "like I was scared a little, but I wanted to tell her about it." The teacher did not ask Heather to explain why she drew God in this way, nor would she listen to what Heather was trying to say. Instead, she crossed out the drawing with her red pen and asked Heather to do it again, "This time, the right way!" (see figure 1).

Figure 1. Heather's Drawing of God with "X" Mark Over Drawing

Heather was stunned, and sat in stiff silence. She remained quietly sitting at her desk for the rest of the class session. When it was time to leave, Henry had to pull his sister from the room. When they left the room, Heather began to walk toward their parents. Henry carried his drawing, his sister's drawing, and the blank piece of paper on which Heather was to make her new drawing.

Neither Heather nor Henry said anything about this to their parents at first. Susan and David noticed that Heather was unusually quiet but thought she might be tired or getting a cold. Heather's mother and father became concerned when Heather, usually a very spontaneous and happy child, remained silent and withdrawn. Her withdrawal was noted also by her regular kindergarten teacher.

Heather would not speak to her parents or regular teacher about what had happened. She would not look at the drawing and made her mother place it on a shelf in the hall closet. Henry tried to tell his parents what had happened, but he was not sure himself, though he was sure how the teacher looked. Their parents thought it best not to make an issue of this with the church school teacher and assumed that Heather would get back to being herself in a few days. After three weeks, they realized that intervention was needed. In the meantime, Heather was not forced to return to church school. When Mrs. Green asked about her, Heather's mother said that she was feeling ill. Heather and Henry stopped playing together as they usually did, and both children felt unhappy about this. But Henry's other routines continued in a fairly normal pattern. Heather's routines all seemed to be affected. She remained withdrawn and sullen.

Susan, after discussion with David, brought Heather in for pastoral therapy. While somewhat apprehensive about it, she was convinced that her daughter needed help. Both parents supported the idea of pastoral therapy for two reasons. First, they wanted to find a context in which faith issues could be discussed and respected. Second, they thought that since everything seemed to point to something that happened in the church school class, a pastoral context would be a good choice.

When Susan and David approached Heather about meeting with someone who could help her talk about her drawing, Heather was quiet. Finally Heather agreed. Heather recalled that her mother had asked her about "talking to a nice person who wants you to smile again." Heather became a bit more relaxed with this prospect. She briefly told her mother that she did not want to see Mrs. Green again because she "hurt me, and she doesn't really own God." Susan did not understand the whole situation but realized the significance of what had happened.

Prior to seeking pastoral therapy, Susan met with the church's minister about the incident. He tried to be supportive of Heather but agreed with the teacher that God's image was Father and male. He argued "that there was no female image of God as Mother." When shown the drawing, he remarked, "Heather will need to learn that God is male and that this does not mean that God does not love and protect her." Though Susan could not state, at that point, her precise frustration with this response, something about it was unsettling to her.

When Susan talked with me a week later, she said:

I don't know why, but the minister's words really left me feeling, well, out of sorts. . . . I have tried to raise Heather and Henry to be good and strong children, inside and out. I never thought much about God in this way, but if Heather can't use her imagination, then maybe she can't really feel God's strength either. I have to say, being a strong Christian, I never questioned anything like this before, but when I see my child being changed like this, I really have prayed and I feel God is leading her here.

II: Moving Through the Episodes of Critical Caring

Therapeutic Timeline

When one is working with a member of a family, especially with a child, consultations and meetings with other family members are often desirable and necessary. In my work with Heather, I met with her mother and father at several points. Though this case study will concentrate on my work with Heather, her family's involvement will be discussed as it relates to Heather's therapeutic movement.

Heather and I worked together over a seven-month period, from mid-October through mid-May, meeting once a week on Friday afternoons. Heather liked Fridays and found Friday afternoons a quiet and happy time. Since my schedule allowed for this, we chose this as our meeting time.

Episode 1. Creation of Safe Therapeutic Space

Creating a safe therapeutic space is as or more important for a child as it is for an adult. Allowing Heather a chance to pick a meeting time was the first step in this safety-creating process. Considering what I had heard from Heather's mother, Heather's critical empowerment and involvement in the space would be essential to making it a safe space.

On her first visit both Heather and her mother came into the room. Heather and I sat cross-legged on the floor. Susan remained in a large chair. Heather found the space comfortable enough to ask me who I was and if she could bring her doll out of the bag. Heather's doll, Molly, became an important resource for our creation of a safe space. At the end of the session, Heather noted, "Molly likes it here and would like to come back." Through Molly, Heather felt it worth the risk to begin claiming the space as her own.

Her doll, Molly, opened the way for Heather to bring in other symbols of her life. During the early sessions I invited Heather to express herself in a variety of ways. Having paper, crayons, a tape player, old clothes, a variety of stuffed animals, and picture books at her disposal, Heather turned to all of these forms with the exception of drawing. At the end of the second session Heather told her mother, "Mommy, you can go read outside from now on. Molly and me will be okay in here. We have lots of things to do."

Her mother smiled and said this would be fine. For Heather, having her voice heard and feeling in control in this sense gave her strength and a renewed vitality. Later in the week Susan called to let me know how much more lively Heather had become and how she told Henry about all of the different things in my office. Heather was claiming the therapeutic space and process. Molly became Heather's link into and out of the therapeutic process.

In the third session Heather said, "I like to make pictures, but not now. It is something special but not now. I have one in the closet but not now." This statement referring to the church school incident signaled Heather's ability to keep the memory of what had happened in her conscious mind but also her grappling with a way to contain the memory until a means for processing it could be found. In this third session, building on the safety of the therapeutic space and trust in the relationship, Heather was able to mention the as-yet unnameable.

Episode 2. Entry Into Symbolic Reality

Heather's activity and love of music and dance, as evidenced in her behavior in the sessions, offered clues to her symbolic reality. Working with Heather and her love of music, and supplementing this with selected conversations with her mother and father, we began to explore Heather's symbolic reality.

Heather and Henry had experienced a stable and supportive environment for their development in a traditional family whose central religious symbols focused on Christianity and the possibilities, as Susan stated, "of a new world taking place, of love on this earth, a world of hope for our children and all children, through the love of Jesus Christ."

Each parent communicated this love, hope, and possibility to both children. Prior to the incident at church, both children seemed happy and balanced at home. Heather and Henry spent much time together and with their parents. But the church school incident marked a significant questioning of this equal love, hope, and possibility. At home, the children observed mother and father working as partners. Both parents worked, though the father assumed more financial responsibility and the mother assumed more responsibility for home and children.

The incident at church school helped surface family tensions and issues that Susan and David had not identified fully and in fact had consciously avoided to this point. Both parents wanted the future open to their children and did not intend to force stereotypical roles on them. The relative openness and encouragement of different possibilities in this family contrasted with the rigid and punitive family structures and expectancies in the biological families of both parents. Explosive anger and moral outbursts characterized Susan's family memories. David's memories were filled with his parents' deafening silences and emotional withdrawals. Both sets of grandparents were alive and visited twice yearly. Susan and David both acknowledged that at those times they and the children felt uncomfortable most of the time. Usual family activities and the children's activities were suspended during grandparents' visits because Susan, David, Heather, and Henry felt the watchful and critical eyes of grandparental judgment. Though Susan and David had expressed frustration in private, they had decided that in order to preserve family tradition and honor, these visits had to continue. They were concerned, however, about the effects on the children and hoped things would get better as the children got older.

Family tensions and the underlying symbolic realities supporting these tensions were brought to light by Heather in our sessions in a variety of ways. Heather talked about feelings for her parents, grandparents, and the different beliefs each had about life. Heather told many stories about the family members. In addition to my time with Heather gathering information on family transitions and tensions, I arranged two sessions with Susan and David. The first was at the request of Susan, as she identified issues surfacing for the family. Susan expressed that she herself was experiencing serious questions in her own faith and her own imaging of God. David was struggling to understand the issues for Susan and agreed to a session with her. At the end of this session, which took place at the end of the second month, other issues surfaced and so another session was scheduled. Though space does not permit discussion of these sessions, they served as an anchor for my time with Heather in two ways. First, Susan and David told Heather and Henry that they wanted to talk about some things with a therapist because, as Susan said, "when something is not going right, it is important to find out what is happening." Heather was relieved that her parents were getting help. She said, "I'm glad that Mommy and Daddy are talking to you, too. Henry doesn't worry about them, but I do sometimes." Second, having a time, as David expressed it, "to get away and talk about something with someone not directly involved," gave Susan and David an outlet that the family as a whole needed. From time to time Susan would have Henry along when she brought Heather to the sessions. At different times I would chat with Henry and sometimes Heather would invite him in to see things in my office. Later on, Henry's involvement would become important, but at this point in the therapeutic relationship it was appropriate for him to be at the margins of the process.

Episode 3. Identifying Central Strategies and Rituals of Symbolic Reality

In our second month together, Heather began to talk about different prayers that she prayed with her family. This began when Heather asked me if I would say a prayer with her and her mother at the beginning of a session. When I said "Yes," she was excited. As the three of us prayed the following family prayer, Heather began to dance. "Bless us, Lord, this we pray. Keep us strong tomorrow and today." The prayer and dance brought two dimensions of Heather together that earlier had been kept separate. Heather had prayed, and she had danced, but she had not done both together. After the prayer and before Susan left, Heather remarked, "I only dance to my prayers when I feel good or really bad. But then it's a different kind of dance."

Over the next month, in my conversations with Heather and through her dances, a profile of rituals and strategies in Heather's symbolic reality emerged. Her family engaged in many religious rituals as part of daily life in-cluding meal prayers, meditation, and a family-focusing prayer time after din-ner. Most prayers began with the phrase "In Jesus' name we pray" or "God, our Father, hear us." Interestingly, though family prayers were begun and ended with references to Jesus or to God as Father, God was not limited to such references in the prayers that Heather prayed in the therapeutic context. Heather remembered praying to God who was like a dancing butterfly: "I made up a song of God as a butterfly, dancing and singing." Heather's par-ents were not aware of the juxtaposition of the fixed prayer introductions and the free rein of divine imagery in Heather's praying prior to the church school incident.

Heather's symbolic reality included the religious rituals of her family and her rituals of play with her dolls. A third and vitally important part of Heather's symbolic reality was her relationship with Henry. As twins, the two children were physically and emotionally close. Each greatly enjoyed their emotional closeness. Heather, born ten minutes before Henry, was the more spontaneous of the two. Henry was the more quiet. The incident in church had led to a disruption of their play rituals. Henry was upset for his sister and wanted to destroy the drawing and forget about it. Heather insisted that the drawing remain in the closet and in the beginning withdrew from drawing and from playing with Henry.

By the third month the therapeutic space had become a safe, ritualizing play space for Heather. Although she could not yet talk about the drawing and did not draw in the sessions, her releasing of energy and increasing com-fortability were signs that in her critically caring way, Heather was claiming this space and performing rituals to make it her own. These included:

> having her mother come in at certain sessions at the end to
> say a special prayer that Heather began with the words,
> "Dear God";
> creating and performing dances for me, whom she called
> "the question lady with the nice laugh";
> having us dance together and sometimes inviting her mother
> when she wanted to dance in order to get, in Heather's
> words, "special energy."

"Special energy" in this context meant energy that Heather needed when she thought about sad or frightening things. This had been one of Heather's creative strategies since age three. Her mother recounted Heather's doing a dance, at age four, with a rhythmic song asking grandma and grandpa to go away. This happened after Heather's maternal grandparents had launched sev-eral outbursts condemning the too permissive ways of parenting and the dan-gers of dance and music for the children's development. From time to time Heather would invite Henry to join in the dance, and although Henry did not conceive of the dance in the same way, he enjoyed being a part of it.

In early December Heather brought her favorite drawing markers to our session. At different times she had brought her favorite dolls, animals, and other special things. Bringing her markers symbolized a degree of trust and direction sufficient for delving into the church school incident. When I asked her why she brought these markers, Heather responded, "Because these are the best ones, and I use them for special things." Heather went to the pile of construction paper and picked out two pieces of white paper. She asked if she could draw, and when I said yes, proceeded to pray a silent prayer with hands folded over the paper. Then she drew an enclosed circle with figures inside. Heather explained that this was a drawing "of my energy circle dance that I told you about." She asked if Henry could come next time and do the dance with her. We agreed that if Henry wanted to, he could come. Heather decided to leave the markers with me.

Heather's progression in therapy—sharing elements of her symbolic world, talking about her special dance, bringing in her special markers, and designing the plan of her energy dance around her markers—brought the healing power of Heather's symbolic world and its rituals into the therapeutic space and relationship. Heather's invitation to Henry to join both in the dance and in her sessions marked her ability to proceed in her exploration of what had happened on *that* Sunday.

At the following session Heather and Henry danced Heather's energy dance, and then both sat on the floor with the markers and construction paper. While Henry drew a picture of the sky and ocean, Heather drew a picture of "a dancing butterfly with wings for everybody." In the session, after Henry left, Heather began to cry and said that she had been thinking about "my drawing in the hall closet." The energy dance, her sharing it with Henry, and their drawings had surfaced the memory of the church school incident, and Heather was a bit surprised at this. "I love the dance and Henry too, and I feel kind of happy but a patch of sad too." She pointed to her drawing of the butterfly and a green-black flowerlike drawing in the bottom. Heather explained that this was her "patch of sad." She was feeling this along with the happy feeling of the dancing butterfly. The following conversation ensued:

V. Do you feel the happy feeling someplace special?

H. Yeh, in my belly, kind of a dancing in there, real good.

V. And what about the sad patch?

H. Oh [brief pause], that is here [pointing to her right shoulder] like a big pack to carry.

V. Can you put the pack down?

H. I want to, but it [pause, thinking] is stuck there.

V. Could the dancing butterfly help?

H. Oh, yeh. It could maybe stay there [pointing to shoulder] and lift it with me.

V. Is the butterfly strong?

H. [excited] Yes, yes, very strong, like a real strong wind, real strong.

V. If you close your eyes and imagine the butterfly on your shoulder, how does it feel?

H. Like a friend, like a friend, it feels good. I like it and feel the wings in my hair.

Episodes 4 and 5. Assessing the Impact of Strategies and Rituals on the Caring Process and Bringing Them Into the Therapeutic Context

The central strategies and rituals in Heather's symbolic reality had worked in a positive way for her growth and development. These found their way into the therapeutic context within the first month. Because Heather used these rituals and strategies so often to bring balance and energy to her life, the challenge emerged for us to find a way to take the balancing and energizing potential of these strategies and rituals to encounter the church school incident: to name it, to make sense of it, and to strategize a way to put it in perspective through containment. The groundwork for this had been laid, and Heather's image of God as the dancing butterfly produced a means of entry. Heather decided to undertake this challenge at a special period in the Christian year, Advent and Christmastide. The natural excitement and tension of this period were complicated by emerging family issues that surfaced in part through Heather's church school experience. Throughout this period, Heather and her family wrestled with questions that challenged their faith and therefore their lives individually and collectively. Heather and her family drew upon the rituals and strategies of their symbolic reality to find the courage and strength to nurture their faith through this period.

The imaging exercise with the butterfly helped Heather to focus her energy in the next several sessions. Toward the end of our second month together, Heather brought her church school drawing with her in a manila envelope. She let me hold the envelope but did not want us to talk about it. Instead, Heather told me about a worry she had with church: "I don't want to go to church for Christmas. Sometimes I see that teacher, and I get kinda sick." This session, taking place two weeks before Christmas, offered evidence that although Heather was not being forced to attend church school, the negative effect of being in that church environment was real. When I asked Heather if she wanted to talk about Christmas, she indicated that she did but also asked if her mother could come in and talk too.

Susan joined us and, with her mother's support, Heather voiced her anxiety about "celebrating" Christmas. The Christmas ritual and season helped focus attention on the ongoing consequences of Heather's church school experience and a growing concern between Heather's parents about church membership. Heather, holding her mother's hand, told me how much she loved Christmas and how she felt special about Christmas. But Heather was not looking forward to the special Christmas service. She said, "I don't feel Jesus is in that church, and my stomach hurts when I am there."

As Heather spoke, her mother began crying. Heather turned to her mother and said, "Mommy, you and Daddy were fighting. I heard." Susan said that she and David had been discussing what to do about church and that Heather had told them she did not want to go to the Christmas service. Susan did not want to force Heather to go. David felt that they needed to go as a family. Both Susan and David were concerned that the church school incident was having too great an effect on Heather. Susan was concerned about how things would get resolved and was clear that she did not want to argue with David about this. Heather and Henry were going away for a few days with their aunt, uncle, and cousins before Christmas. I asked Susan if she and David could come in for a session while the children were away.

The session with Susan and David focused on the Christmas day decision but allowed both parents to express their concerns. David expressed concern for what had happened with Heather but hoped she would be able to "get over it and get things back to normal." He admitted that the changes in Heather were strong but felt that was part of Heather's personality. Susan also expressed concern but understood the situation somewhat differently: "I don't think Heather will get 'over this,' David. It's like a big thing to her, and maybe we should see what forcing her would do to hurt her."

The tension level began rising silently, and Susan asked if we could pray. David agreed. They recited together a prayer they had written years before. The visible calming effect of prayer for Susan and David was similar to the effect of dance and the energy circle for Heather. After the prayer, I asked Susan and David if they could think about what to do for Christmas itself and see if a short-term compromise could be reached. Susan suggested that they go to a service at another church so as not to force Heather on this issue. She suggested a local church that she had been to for lay-leadership training sessions. David thought it important not to be in a "strange place" for Christmas. After some discussion, each trying to respect the other's concerns, Susan and David decided that they would go to two Christmas services, one at their regular church and the other at the church Susan suggested. This seemed to them to be a way of negotiating David's understanding of the need for "familiarity and belonging" and Susan's understanding of the need for "respect and noncoercion." They planned to tell Henry and Heather of this plan when the children returned.

The next scheduled session was in January, marking the third month of the therapeutic process with Heather. Prior to the session Susan called to let me know that the plan had worked pretty well but that other issues were surfacing. On the day of the session, Heather was eager to tell me many things. She set the agenda with the words, "Boy, so much to tell you. Me and Molly really had adventures." Clearly, Heather's words indicated her preparation and anticipation of returning to the therapeutic process, a process she trusted and shared.

Heather began by telling me about her vacation with her cousins, and how she and Henry played with their toys. She was also excited to tell me about her Christmas presents, especially her new bicycle. She said, "It was a good Christmas, and Henry and I got to go to two churches. I liked the new one. They had a little play, and some of us got to play Jesus. I wanted to be Jesus, but Henry didn't, so he played a shepherd." Heather talked about other things in the service, and about the singing. However, she kept returning to her playing Jesus:

H. They had this big little cradle, and when I was Jesus I liked all of the animals around me.

V. What was the best thing about playing Jesus?

H. Well, it felt so special, and I could help all the children and animals.

V. Were they sick or hurt?

H. Well, maybe. But I mean I could give out hope to them and peace and make things better.

V. What did it feel like inside?

H. Well, um, good. They had this big candle behind the cradle, and I felt warm like the candle. I was happy, and it was hard to keep still.

This experience at the other church gave Heather a perspective from which to experience the second Christmas service at her regular church. Heather commented, "The service was boring, and I stayed behind my Mom most of the time." The excitement that Heather experienced through the first service helped her to "get through this one." Toward the end of the session, Heather motioned toward the envelope with her drawing in it, which was on a shelf. She said, "I want to look at that next time, okay?" I agreed, and Heather left.

Prior to the next session with Heather, I had a session with her parents. Both Susan and David noted the difference in Heather at the first Christmas service. Difficulty arose over their responses to this. Susan wanted to attend the new church, while David felt uncertain and thought it disloyal to leave their regular church. In addition to this tension in deciding the next step, both parents noted that Henry was growing restless and was now saying that he did not want to attend church school either. At the end of the session Susan and David reached a temporary solution. Susan would go with Heather and Henry to services at the new church. David was undecided. I encouraged them to talk to the new minister together as David had suggested.

Two weeks following the session with Susan and David, I met again with Heather. Heather was eager to talk about her visit with "Mommy and Henry to the new church. It was nice, the place where I played Jesus for Christmas. And Mommy let us go to see the school part too. I liked the teacher. She liked my Jesus story. Henry and me played a lot too."

Heather talked on about this experience. Clearly, the impact on her was strong and positive. These two experiences at the new church became critically important new memories through which she found a way to return to her original church school experience and the imaging of God.

Months four and five focused on Heather's journey of return to the church school experience. We began this journey with Heather doing her energy dance, followed by her imaging the butterfly. When Heather felt ready, she got the envelope from the shelf, opened it, and took out her drawing. She stood silently and looked at it. When I asked her if she remembered it looking the way it did, she said, "Well, yeh, but I don't look the same."

V. What do you look like now?

H. I look happier, when I look at it now.

Through this exchange, Heather was able to express a complex transition that was taking place inside her. This transition was from the little girl who had been shamed into hiding her work and hiding herself from herself, to a little girl who could look at herself and understand that it was a different "I" looking at it. The memory of shame and its consequences were being confronted by a memory of acceptance.

During the next several sessions, Heather approached the drawing in different ways. Each time I encouraged her natural inclination to create and recreate a safe context in which to look at the drawing. Heather accomplished this using different activities: her energy dance, singing, inviting her mother to pray with her, and bringing in certain special things. Each time Heather did this, she created the necessary distance from the drawing to be able to look at it without being absorbed into it or absorbing it into her. Her special rituals in the therapeutic context created a psychospatial perspective from which to explore the drawing. These rituals together with the new memories of her different church experience created a spiritual and psychological container for Heather.

In the course of these sessions, Heather went through a four-step approach to the drawing: (1) critical distance, (2) cautious calm, (3) healing anger, and (4) creating future.

1. Critical distance. Heather approached the drawing as though it were encased in a special shield, protecting her from coming too close. She placed it on the floor and walked around it. She looked at and pointed to the drawing but did not touch it. Heather's prayer focused on God as protector: "Save me, Jesus, and don't let me cry."

2. Cautious calm. Heather circled the drawing and asked me to pick it

up with her. She began to cry. The safety of the therapeutic space and relationship allowed her both physically and psychologically to get closer to the drawing and touch it and to touch the pain inside. Heather's prayer focused on God as companion: "Come, Jesus, hold my hand like Mommy does."

3. Healing anger. Heather circled the drawing and began to throw crayons at it. Then she began to cry. Finally she knelt down beside it and hit it with her fist. Heather's prayer to God focused on God as container of her emotions: "Spirit Jesus, this [pointing to drawing] is you, but she made me feel so bad and told me a lie about you. I hate her. She made me hate you. But I love you."

4. Creating future. Heather brought in a new drawing to the next session in an envelope (see figure 2). She calmly placed the envelope next to the original drawing. She walked around them and in silence opened the envelope and placed her new drawing next to the old one.

She began to describe the new drawing to me:

Figure 2. Heather's Drawing of God as a Dancing Butterfly

See, there's me [pointing to a flower], and the butterfly is God. And we are dancing around God's face, and everybody is in God's face. It's the same God as in my other one, but God can dance now. I hate this red X [pointing to the red mark made by Mrs. Green, the church school teacher, on her first drawing]. My butterfly God won't ever have an X on it. I wouldn't put an X on her drawing. God doesn't like what she did. It was not good. God is free now, not staying in the closet anymore.

After describing the new drawing, Heather picked up both drawings, brought them over to me, and asked if I could make a copy and send the new one to her former church school teacher. When I said that I could, she said, "She may not want it, but I want to send it to her, and to my cousins, too. They will like it. She doesn't understand, but maybe God can help her."

Heather's ability to create a new drawing and to set it in juxtaposition to the original allowed her to name and contain the church school incident. Her desire to send it to Mrs. Green marked her success in containing the incident and setting it in perspective in order to be free to express her faith through her new image of God.

Episode 6. Developing Means for Creating New Memory, New Ritual

Over the course of several months, Heather's family made the decision to attend the new church as a family. Reluctantly, Heather's father agreed to go. He did not attend as regularly as Heather's mother and the children, but he was beginning to understand the impact and consequences of the theological beliefs of the two churches. The rhythm of the family's grappling with the family church issue worked well with Heather's rhythm through her cycle of naming and containing. As Heather went through her four-step cycle in therapy, her parents noticed an observable change in Heather's level of energy at home. She began to play with Henry, and she began dancing around the house in her usual way.

In my consultation with Heather's family, they supported Heather's desire to make a copy of her drawing and send it to the teacher and to the minister. In addition to the drawing, her parents sent a letter and helped Heather to write the following note:

> Dear Mrs. Green,
>
> This is a drawing I made. I want you to have a copy. God helped me in this drawing. God is the butterfly and flies around all people. Everybody in the whole world has God's face. No red marks on anyone. I hope you like this.
>
> Love,
> Heather

In the seventh month of therapy there were three sessions. The first included all family members. Heather and her parents wanted to have a time together. Henry had indicated interest in this as well. Henry's interest in meeting together came about when Henry and Heather began playing again in their usual fashion. While Heather had worked through her issues, Henry had by choice remained on the outside of the process. Now as Heather was reentering their world of play, Henry needed to sort through some things and be brought up to date on Heather's and the family's rhythms.

The family met over two sessions, with the first session designed as a family conversation focused on, as David noted, "anything the kids, Susan, or I want to get info on or work out." The family, as a family, appeared calm and happy, in contrast to earlier meetings. Each member came with an agenda. Heather wanted to "show my new drawing and talk about the letter I sent." Henry wanted "to know that Heather is okay and that it is really okay with Daddy to be in the new church." Susan wanted to "share praise and thanks to God that I and David and the children have a new church home." And David wanted "to have us move on and enjoy life again." The agenda items worked well together. We followed, in the sessions, the same ritual pattern that the family used at home when they had their family meetings. Each person had a chance to speak and be heard. True to her ritual form, Heather engaged in an energy dance and asked Henry and her parents to join her.

Before the second session I encouraged Susan and David to talk again with their new minister as they felt it appropriate and to discuss the family changes with him. They met with him and found it helpful and planned to meet with him again to discuss church membership. The minister was very supportive of them and the children and expressed, as Susan put it, "outright grief over what had happened to Heather." Susan and David asked if I might want to talk with him, too, and said they would like that if I could.

Prior to my last session with Heather I did speak with the minister, who was very supportive of Heather and her family. He offered to meet with me and the family if that were ever necessary again. The offer gave hope and strength to all of the family members and to me as a pastoral colleague.

Heather and I planned our last session with care. She wanted to have Molly, her drawings, and other "things here too so I can make a memory." During the session Heather danced a new dance that she had choreographed just for this special occasion. We had a special fruit punch and gingerbread cookies that she baked. When I asked her what I might bring, she said, "Oh, well, some cups, but you need to think what you want to make a memory of too." Indeed, Heather was right, and I brought one of my rag dolls to the celebration. We ended the session with Heather's prayer:

Dear God, thank you for the flowers and people and my Mommy and Daddy and Henry and dancing and Molly and this day. I am sad to not be here after today. I like this lady. But I am happy too that you love me and I can draw you again and dance. God bless us and [pointing to me] her too, and this nice happy room and love.

CHAPTER 5

The Case of Laura: Responsible Anger Giving Birth to Respect

I. Overview and Background

At the time of our meeting, Laura is a twenty-one-year-old woman from a middle-class Caucasian family. She is in her third year of study at a large university. Her major is history. She is an honors student. Laura grew up in a large city on the East Coast. She describes herself with the phrase, "I am smart and ugly." This descriptive phrase was given to Laura by her father and echoed by her mother and two older sisters. Her parents praised her sisters, Evelyn and Mary, for their slightly above-average academic performance. But they expected Laura to perform well above average, saying, "It's academic achievement, the only thing you've got going for you. You better never slip up, or you'll never get a man."

Family of Origin Information

These words of Laura's father were one of the ways in which Laura characterized her childhood. Her family, ninth-generation Americans, came from England, Scotland, and Holland. Laura's family of origin stressed traditional roles for men and women. Her father was a successful banker. Her mother was primarily a homemaker. Both mother and father placed a very high degree of emphasis on physical beauty for women. This pattern of female valuation had been a legacy from Laura's grandmother. In the constellation of family life, Laura's sisters had inherited great physical beauty. Laura had been gifted with a high degree of intelligence and creativity. However, being female and being less than beautiful had made other gifts secondary or unimportant for her family. Laura carried a tremendous burden which crushed her and from which she felt unable to find release as long as she existed in her family context. Laura felt unrelated to her older sisters, being separated from the next oldest by four years. She experienced herself as a virtual stranger in her family.

Being bright, articulate, and creative, Laura had been able to assess her situation even as a young child. And her assessment, from age four, had been that she was "a failure, a disappointment, and a child better left unborn." She frequently dismissed her gifts because at home they had no context for being valued. Although Laura had grandparents on both sides living in different parts of the country, none lived nearby. Therefore, she did not have the chance to develop a close relationship with them. Laura existed primarily within her nuclear family, in a context where there was little room for diversity.

It was a childhood of competition, of never being able to achieve what "women were to be about." As a child, Laura was a loner and felt rejected by her sisters and her parents because she was not beautiful. She was also taunted by her classmates because of her exceptional intelligence. Living in the context of her home, Laura secretly hoped that one day she would become beautiful like her sisters and was more than willing to "give up some intelligence to do so."

As a teenager, Laura rebelled against her family. At thirteen, for the first time in her life, she began to do poorly in school. At this time as well she began to turn her attention "to anything that would get me the attention of boys and men." She saw herself as "promiscuous and popular with several boys at school and in my neighborhood." Though at fifteen her school work seemed to improve, she continued her promiscuous behavior. At first her parents did not know what was happening. Once they discovered her behavior, they ostracized Laura all the more.

At seventeen Laura discovered that she was pregnant. She did not know who the father was, and she felt quite alone. Prior to learning of the pregnancy, Laura's mother in desperation had taken her to the minister of their local Methodist church for help. Laura, to her mother's surprise, did not resist going. She had hoped that somehow through talking with someone she might be able to understand and come to terms with things. She acknowledged that she felt confused inside. As a young child Laura had been intrigued by the idea of God and Jesus. She liked Jesus, especially as he was presented through the church school readings from the Bible. He always seemed to care, in her words, "for the ugly ones."

Laura requested that she see the minister alone because she did not want her mother to hear what she had to say. Her mother agreed. Over the course of five sessions the minister asked Laura several direct questions about her sexual activity, parental disobedience, and the right things for girls to do. Laura answered all the questions but "felt abandoned by God." At seventeen she felt that "very little real care was offered in this pastoral care and that he [the minister] didn't understand my pain, my deep pain." Her mother wanted her to return to see the minister, but Laura refused. Laura at this time discovered that she was pregnant. She felt abandoned and dreaded what her parents might say about the pregnancy.

At first she tried to hide the pregnancy through a pattern of overeating. She hoped that somehow she could be sent away without her parents finding out about the pregnancy. A friend of hers, a girl from high school, went with her to be tested and was trying to work with Laura to find a way out of the pregnancy. In desperation in her third month of pregnancy, Laura finally told her parents: "I confessed to my parents that I was pregnant and that I wanted to keep the baby." Her parents, especially her father, insisted that she could not do that. He informed her that her only choices were to abort the child or to give it up for adoption. He preferred abortion. Laura's mother was silent, which was her way of responding when her husband made a decision. Neither of Laura's sisters offered any opinion and in fact had, in a functional sense, dissociated themselves from Laura several years before. Laura asked if she might talk to the associate minister at church who was female. Her mother consented but demanded that Laura not discuss the pregnancy. Laura had two sessions with the female minister and consciously avoided the topic of her pregnancy.

Laura did not comment to me on the content of her conversations with the female minister and did not seem to remember very much of it. What she did remember, however, was that instead of being asked questions about her behavior, the female minister asked her questions about Laura, her happiness, and what led her to do damage to herself in certain ways. This had a very profound impact on Laura. Though, at her mother's insistence, she did not continue in conversation with the female minister, Laura felt that a seed of hope had been planted. The seed was quite simply that she had permission to ask questions about herself. For Laura this was a revelation. She had never been aware that one could ask God questions about oneself and that God would accept those questions. Laura felt that somehow, though she did not know how, she could try to move forward with her life even though she felt she had greatly sinned.

Three weeks after her last meeting with the female minister Laura's parents took her to an abortion clinic, and her pregnancy was terminated. The family never discussed this experience. It was considered a closed topic, shrouded with disapproval and guilt. Laura bore her guilt, her shame, her anger at herself, and her anger at her parents in silence. Though she had one close female friend with whom she had shared things before, Laura thought it wise to try to bury all things associated with the abortion, including her emotions and memories.

Laura spent the last semester of her junior year and her senior year in high school losing herself in her work. Her exceptional mind surfaced again, and not only was she able to be admitted to every university to which she applied, but she was also offered substantial financial support. Laura chose a large university that allowed her to be geographically separated from her family. She hoped that somehow in another context she could find a way to work through all the layers of emotions and memories that she had very deliberately and out of psychological necessity buried.

During Laura's first two years at the university she excelled in her studies. She also went, from time to time, to a women's support group. Although she remained silent in the group, they welcomed her. She felt strongly that she needed something, some kind of context or support, in order to begin looking at what had happened in her life. However, she also knew that she was not ready yet to talk, and this was respected. In her sophomore and junior years at college, she began attending the university's chapel services. Of the five chaplains, Laura found herself gravitating toward a female chaplain who came out of the United Methodist tradition. Prior to Laura's coming to pastoral psychotherapy, she had two conversations with the female chaplain. Laura felt that attending chapel and working with the chaplain might be something that would make sense for her. She looked forward to future meetings with the chaplain, who helped Laura find a pastoral context on which to base her therapy. Laura expressed her reasoning as follows, "I have a need and desire to understand things both in my past and for my life now through my faith."

Religious Background

Laura's family belonged to a medium-sized United Methodist congregation. The family was a strong economic contributor to the church and was considered to be a model family in the community. The congregation consisted of professionals and nonprofessionals. Laura's parents set high standards for themselves and for their place in the church. For example, Laura remembered one Sunday in particular when her mother could not locate a particular pair of shoes. She caused such a scene and created so much disturbance that the family did not go to church because to go with a different pair would have been inappropriate for church attendance. The standards, physical or otherwise, set by her parents were absolute. All family members had to conform.

Laura's personal experiences in church school and worship were different from her parents' experience. She found, especially through reading scripture and singing hymns, a release that she did not feel at home. Being a Methodist, she was exposed to the hymns of Charles Wesley. She remembered as a young child going through the hymnal which featured a great many of Wesley's hymns. She found the words of these hymns and their melodies soothing. They helped form her image of God.

This image focused on a God of love, compassion, forgiveness, and most of all companionship. She was far less aware of the image of God portrayed from the pulpit during those times that she sat in church with her parents. Laura's church school image of God was fairly consistent with the image Wesley portrayed. Through reading and music, Laura found her theology and image of God developing. Laura asked her church school teacher if she could take the hymnal home and her teacher wisely agreed. Laura recalled that many times as a child when she felt either neglected or lonely at home she would go to her room, sit on her bed, open the hymnal, and begin singing. Though as a young child Laura did not comprehend all of the hymns, the act of singing them in her room and feeling a connection with God allowed Laura to find some hope and balance in her life. As she sang, she imagined Jesus as a source of love, compassion, forgiveness, and companionship. These images helped her create a microworld within her family's world.

Through her very difficult adolescence, Laura continued this strategy of hymn singing and God imaging. Between fifteen and seventeen Laura composed her own hymns, which she never shared with anyone. This strategy and the use of her energy in this way helped her to keep some sense of balance. When Laura realized that her abortion was inevitable, she wrote a special hymn, begging God's forgiveness and God's companionship as she prepared for the procedure. Her hymn included the following lines:

> God, Jesus, keep me safe,
> Take my hand and touch my soul,
> You are my strength, you are my life,
> Forgive me my sins and
> What I must face.

Laura described this hymn-writing episode as the pivotal act of faith that kept her from committing suicide as she faced the prospect of losing her fetus and a part of herself. As she survived that very difficult and traumatic point in her life, she became more aware of the difference between her faith and that of her parents. She believed that it would have been possible and healing to speak with the female minister in her church about the pregnancy, but she felt she could not override her parents' decision that it must remain a secret. Laura hoped that at some future point she could talk about the abortion and find a sense of resolution and forgiveness with God through her faith. The memory that Laura carried and the hope that she had harbored from age seventeen brought Laura to search for a faith-related context for therapy at age twenty-one.

II. Moving Through the Episodes of Critical Caring

Therapeutic Timeline

My work with Laura extended over a seventeen-month period. During this time Laura moved from the second half of her junior year into the completion of her senior year at the university.

Episode 1. Creation of Safe Therapeutic Space

Laura was both eager and cautious in her approach to the therapeutic process. She was eager in the sense that she had felt calm enough to begin therapy, having gone through two-and-a-half years at the university, away from home. She felt stable in her studies and had created for herself a different reality than what she had lived at home. She had done a great deal of work to seek out a pastoral therapist with whom to work. On the other hand, the very thought of becoming vulnerable in the therapeutic process created a hesitancy and a caution in Laura, accompanied by a heightened sense of anxiety. Creating a safe therapeutic space and a safe therapeutic relationship took place over a two-month period. Laura was very interested in working from a therapeutic model and doing, as she expressed it, "my own work with a model for help." Laura's studies helped in the creation of a safe space. Her major was history, her minor music. At our initial consultation, Laura appeared positive and re-laxed as she described her work. She noted, "When I am doing my work here, studying and research and all that, I feel most at home." Laura's identification of these areas as ones that helped her to feel comfortable made possible a posi-tive connection between Laura and the therapeutic space. Laura was a bit sur-prised and skeptical that there could be such a connection. However, the idea of bringing her positive studies into the therapeutic space and having them in some way work as a point of entry for her made her very excited. At the end of the first session she expressed a natural anticipation of our meeting again. She closed the session by saying, "Maybe my life can be like a historical study, and I can write some music to describe the points in my life."

From our second meeting onward Laura and I named, discussed, and found ourselves comfortable with the creative roles of "investigators." We were investigating the formation, in Laura's words, "of this bridge between my present world and my studies." Laura thought this bridge might help her feel "at home" in the therapeutic space and the translation of that into the therapeutic relationship. Over these two months, as Laura became more at ease, she began to create links for herself in terms of identifying what felt safe about her studies and why she very deliberately chose these as her areas. She came to see that there was nothing haphazard in her choices of history and music. In the second month of our work, Laura began to create rather elabo-rate charts for the different periods in her life, using her historical methods. At the same time, between sessions, Laura returned to singing, especially the hymns of Wesley, while sitting at the piano in the music lab.

At the end of the second month Easter was upon us, and Laura felt it important that she attend Easter service at the chapel. She already had made the decision that she would not return home for Easter break. Laura wanted to devote this time to the therapeutic process and felt that this would be an important time for her. I encouraged Laura not only to attend the Easter ser-vice as an important marker of her faith but also to see if she could find a time to meet with the Protestant chaplain with whom she had felt some connection earlier. Laura was enthusiastic about this and in fact was able to arrange a meeting.

By the end of the second month, several dimensions of the creation of a safe space and a responsible therapeutic relationship had been achieved. First, Laura was able to identify and bring into the therapeutic space those resources in her life, her historical studies and her love of music, which she felt could help her in and through her therapeutic process. Second, the timing of the therapy in conjunction with Easter assisted Laura to connect the therapeutic process with Easter and its symbolism of death and resurrection. Third, pastoral therapy, with its understanding of faith and the importance of working through theological symbols, allowed her to make connections among her therapeutic work, her new community of faith, and her interaction with the Protestant chaplain.

Episode 2. Entry Into Symbolic Reality

This stage of the therapeutic process took place over a four-month period. Entering Laura's past symbolic reality meant entering through three levels of that reality: her relationship with her family, her relationship with her church and church school, and the symbolic reality Laura herself created through her music and the singing of hymns in her room at home.

We began entry by starting with this third level, the world that she created for herself in her room at home. Starting here was an intentional choice since Laura considered this to be a safer space than the space with her family. It was clear that exploring Laura's symbolic reality with her family would raise many traumatic memories for her. Starting this exploration at a safer level allowed us to move cautiously from episode one to two. The safe space we had established in the therapeutic context provided a new memory of safety for Laura. It helped her to name her need in childhood to create a safe place of refuge.

Laura's ability to name the need for such a place helped her to recall memories of her room. She strongly associated this place with singing the Wesley hymns and reading the New Testament. Her memories became vivid and very sharp. Laura's earliest memory of such activities was around the age of five when she received from her grandmother a small piano. "It was somewhere between a toy and a real thing, and I kept it in my room." At this young age Laura played music though she could not as yet read music from the hymnal. Through her excellent sense of pitch and tone, she was able to decipher tunes of the hymns that she had sung in church. Within her room Laura was able to create an atmosphere of relative peace: "my safer space," as she named it.

This level of Laura's symbolic reality, the creation of her "safer space," was linked directly to a second level, the symbolic reality of the church and her church school experiences. These experiences helped to provide the resources for her "safer space" in terms of music and hymns. Though her attendance at church diminished as she approached her teenage years, church remained a life-giving resource. At the second level, Laura felt for the most part free of destructive judgment and condemnation. This contrasted sharply with the values and feelings in the symbolic reality of Laura's parents. At the third level, her parents' reality, Laura felt herself "as being deficient and wanting, with little or no hope for ever changing my 'status' in their world." Laura remembered her father telling her, "You are only a female and not even a pretty one." Laura experienced her parents' theology and image of God consonant with this kind of approach to reality: "God was rigid and stern. The categories of sin were set, and the lines of judgment were inflexible." Her parents, from Laura's perspective, seemed to hold themselves as accountable and as subject to judgment as they did Laura. This judgment was translated into other parts of their life as well. Laura felt that her sisters fared much better in this type of symbolic reality because from birth they were gifted with the "right" gifts for females: beauty, charm, and grace. Laura just started out "wrong." Over this four-month time period Laura found it helpful to create a number of charts (see figure 3).

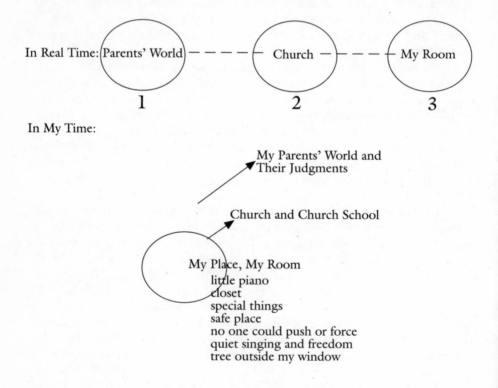

Figure 3. Laura's Three Levels of Symbolic Reality from Her Past

In these charts, relying on her historical method, Laura traced these three different levels of her symbolic reality. As the chart indicates, Laura distinguished between chronological time and symbolic time, and she deciphered the impact of places and meaning in her life. Seeing them on paper helped her to name and locate the experiences of pain and of hope that she endured in the symbolic world of her past.

Episode 3. Identifying Central Strategies and Rituals of Symbolic Reality

Working through the third episode took place over a five-month period. Our work during this time took place as Laura went from the end of her junior year through the summer and into her senior year of college. During this period our weekly meetings continued, with a less frequent schedule during the summer. Laura chose to stay in the area and work at a local job in order to continue with the therapeutic process. Our change in schedule over the summer was arranged to accommodate certain exercises that we were doing in therapy.

The chart (figure 3) of the three levels of Laura's past symbolic reality proved very useful for us in identifying central strategies and rituals. Laura found it helpful to take each of these levels—the "safer space" in her room, the heritage and inheritance of her worship and church school experience, and the world of her parents—and think about the different strategies and rituals that took place in each. Laura found it comforting, balancing, and empowering to use this kind of charting. It gave her a means for naming and sorting, two functions Laura needed. Sometimes she would do her charting and then visit the music lab. She would create different musical scores as she was going through the recall process. With some frequency Laura would bring in musical tapes to go along with charts. Through these resources Laura identified a strategy in her present that assisted her access and sorting of memory.

Movement into this third episode of the therapeutic process was accomplished through her present strategies of charting and musical composing. In placing herself back in the context of her safer space within her own room as a child, Laura remembered particular rituals she performed and experienced. When she was going to begin her hymn-singing process on her bed, she would prepare her bed by placing there certain pillows, her very favorite stuffed animals, and one particular doll. Laura sensed, even as a young child, that certain activities done for certain reasons needed to be approached with care. She was fastidious about the ritual around her hymn singing. Laura also recalled another ritual of care in her approach to her piano. In her early church experience Laura found the ritual of worship very important. As a child this special time on Sunday morning, both in worship and in church school, was comfortable and renewing. She identified the singing of hymns and the reading of scripture as pivotal points. All of these rituals involved positive religious and spiritual dimensions. In and through them Laura received caring that helped her to survive the experiences of humiliation and destruction.

Her parents' symbolic reality and its strategies and rituals were painful but vivid memories for Laura. One very traumatic ritual took place on a Sunday morning prior to church when all the women in the family were working to make themselves "beautiful and attractive for God," as Laura's mother would say. Laura felt herself going through this ritual as though "I was being pulled away from myself, being destroyed bit by bit." The contrast of this negative ritual followed by the powerful and positive ritual of church and church school was important.

As we began the summer, knowing that she had decided to remain in the geographical area, she wanted to work on specific assignments and ways in which she could know best how to recover more of her memories. Laura did journaling, spent two hours every day with her music, and wrote poems. Each of these gave her a rhythm and a sense of security that facilitated memory recall. At this point in our work the positive tension of moving between past memory recall and present strategies was important for Laura. As her present strategies gained momentum, she was able to gain increased access to the music lab over the summer. We concentrated on her work in music. Laura was able to write to her home church and ask a former church school teacher to send her one of the older hymnals that they used when she attended the church. It was important to have the hymnal itself and to go back through the strategy of hymn singing, especially Wesley's hymns, that had been such a powerful resource for her. Over the summer she did a great deal of work between meetings through recovery of hymns and other strategies and rituals that she had developed earlier. This brought us into the middle of August. At this time memories surfaced surrounding Laura's teenage years.

Strategies and rituals in all three dimensions of her life changed dramatically at the time when she became sexually active. As Laura described it, "This time I used my body and sex for all the wrong things. I needed love and attention. And as I became sexually promiscuous, I felt estranged from my body altogether." A consequence of this was that Laura began to punish her body and herself for being less than adequate in her parents' eyes, for being less than adequate in God's eyes, and for being less than adequate in her own eyes. Laura's felt need to abuse her body coupled with her need for male attention and response worked to bring her close to self-destruction. She was alienated from her parents. She stopped attending church. This was a period and pattern of withdrawal.

Laura's self-destructive behaviors can be understood as ritual activities in themselves with very destructive consequences. If we refer to rituals as "co-evolved symbolic acts" (see page 44), then Laura's sexual and other destructive behaviors can be approached in this way. Her body became a symbolic object from which Laura needed to be estranged. Her sexual activities became ritual activities that led to a ritual pattern of abuse. As the pattern of estrangement emerged and intensified, Laura found herself out of control and overtaken by the activities themselves. As often happens in such situations, Laura created a conscious means of evaluating and distancing whereby she felt punishment of her body and herself was necessary for her very survival. This conscious punishment created some means of containment for her situation, which had evolved to the point where control was no longer a possibility. The nature of her behaviors and internal patterns of punishment and condemnation could not help but have a strong impact on the strategies and rituals in Laura's "safer space."

During this time, therefore, her strategies and rituals in her "safer space" also changed dramatically. Laura remembered placing the hymnal on the top shelf of her bookcase and sealing her small piano with tape. For more than a year, from fourteen to fifteen, Laura did not touch her music, and "I wouldn't let the music touch me either." Laura clearly recalled her teenage awareness of withdrawal from the positive strategies and rituals that she had created. At the same time she recalled the feeling of "throwing myself into activities that were negative for me."

Laura remembered the turbulence of this teenage period as trying to combat the "spiraling downwards of me and all I had been able to hold together." The two positive areas of ritual, her church and "safe space" experience, were not strong enough to battle the impact of what was happening to her. They could not contain the tensions and struggles both within and outside of Laura. She found herself consciously distancing her mind from her body.

Laura remembered her first experience of menstruation and the way in which she tried to hide it from everyone, especially herself. She did not talk about it with her parents, her sisters, or any of her friends. She went through that developmental ritual in secrecy. At the same time Laura found her body changing. Although she intellectually understood that these changes needed to be happening, she did not know psychologically or spiritually how to prepare herself. Laura recalled feeling awkward and lost during this period. She remembered becoming more and more distant from and disgusted by her own body. Laura continued to struggle with her deep need for physical closeness and intimacy. She described this agonizing dilemma in this way: "I felt repulsed by myself, by my body, and yet I also felt the need for touch and love in my body."

Laura's attempt to resolve this repulsion-need dilemma found its expression in her initial sexual encounters with boys of her age and later with men. Reflecting on the period from fourteen through seventeen, Laura remembered having "more sexual encounters than I can bear to think." She described them as "encounters not always hostile but which I endured." What she endured was not necessarily physical pain, but "it was the pain that I could not feel who I was or why I was doing this." At the same time, these experiences "did give me some desperate sense of being comforted at the surface." When she was seventeen Laura became pregnant. She was not certain by which man she had become pregnant.

As Laura began to remember her past in the therapy context, she found herself remembering it in a different way:

> I thought about these memories in the past, and they are bad memories. Now I am seeing that these things I did were because of things around me and not just because I was a bad person. Like these rituals I did. I never thought of them like this in the past. It helps, it really helps me understand them and get more distance from them in my mind.

Laura needed to remember and rename in order not to get consumed by her past. During this time in therapy Laura attended chapel for daily prayer and requested prayer in our sessions. She was anxious about remembering her pregnancy and all the trauma surrounding it. Laura worked hard to keep her perspective in the present. During our sessions we used prayer and hymn singing to keep the present alive. These religious activities engaged all of Laura. They kept her from being pulled into past pain. When she felt this happening, she prayed aloud or in silence. In this way she literally stopped herself, gained strength and perspective, and, when it was safe, continued. Respecting and trusting this process of critical self-intervention, Laura was able to continue her identification and naming of past rituals.

Laura now recognized that during her teenage period, when her former rituals no longer worked for her, she replaced them with the "ritual of sex." The sex ritual brought little if any physical pleasure but it did accomplish, for a brief period of time, being in contact with another human being. While Laura was pregnant and before the enforced abortion, Laura did not engage in sexual activity. She returned to her ritual of hymn singing in the safe space of her room. By enforcing Laura's isolation from the church and from her friends, her family gave Laura very little space in which to move. However, Laura remembered this period of being in her room and returning to her hymn singing as being genuinely helpful. She wanted to create this safer space for the child developing inside her as well. Laura believed that whereas she viewed her own physical body with disgust and mistrust, this life within her was innocent and one through which she might be able to find something that she had lost. Laura fought against the abortion but finally stopped resisting: "I just stopped fighting and figured I would be dead soon too." Following the abortion, Laura continued to use the rituals of her safer space. Laura felt almost no connection with her body after the abortion.

Laura now understood, in the therapeutic context, how she had marked her development and what strategies and rituals she had developed during the year after the abortion. She lived at home for a year finishing her school work and applying to universities. During that year she spent time in her room or at the library. She was very isolated but not as repulsed by herself as she had been. During that period she spoke very little if at all to her sisters and became virtually mute around her parents. She twice went back to visit the female minister at the church but did not speak about the abortion.

Laura expanded her rituals of music and hymn singing. Once again her room became the safer space. Her room became the transitional space between Laura and the outside world. She now recognized the centrality of her room and her music to her survival. "I guess they held me away from dying. It frightens me now to realize how little I had holding me to life." Many months before she left for the university, Laura began packing. Her ability to survive the year was aided by her commitment to leaving. Laura's choice of university was made on several grounds, with distance from home being an important one. Laura remembered her determination "to take 'off hold' what I had put 'on hold' for so many years when I was at home."

Episode 4. Assessing the Impact of Strategies and Rituals on the Caring Process

For Laura the assessing of these strategies and rituals of her past and present took place over a two-month period. The identification and naming of the strategies and rituals had brought with it a great deal of the assessing process. Being the type of person who by nature analyzed and approached things trying to diagram or chart them, the assessing process for Laura followed on the heels of identifying and naming the rituals. In naming her childhood ritual experiences, including the three dimensions of home, worship, and her safer space, Laura saw clearly the impact of each. The rituals from her home, her parents' symbolic reality, were rituals that had a very disturbing impact on Laura's ability to care. She had no hope of meeting their expectations or standards. In their evaluation Laura could hope for no improvement. In the rituals of worship and church school, Laura found support for her ability to care for God, herself, and others. Through these supportive rituals, Laura found resources that played the most critical part in her psychological and spiritual sanity. Through worship she found music, and this led her to develop rituals in her safer space within her room.

Assessing the impact of her teenage rituals was more difficult and complicated. Laura could identify and name the physiological process of what went on inside as she began to develop into womanhood. It was more difficult and painful to assess the emotional and spiritual confrontations with her body and the ritual of sex that she engaged in to address her repulsion and intimacy needs. It was critically important at this point in therapy for Laura to hear my support for her past need to develop an outlet, a ritual of release, at that point in her life.

This support allowed her freedom to better understand what led her to this ritual of destruction, sexual promiscuity. My support helped Laura now to feel, in her words, "a link to being supported by God. Feeling not okay but for the first time not alone in all this. I had a dream that God understood me and didn't want me to be paralyzed by what I had done not really knowing why." Laura came to understand that she had been inundated and over-whelmed. This led to her release in the destructive sex ritual. In remembering this ritual, especially in understanding the psychological and spiritual need for a ritual of release, Laura finally could name and understand the destructiveness of the ritual without getting lost in its memory.

Laura found my support difficult to understand and accept at first. Months later she remarked on its importance. The therapeutic experience began to give her unconscious and conscious mind ways to counter the perspective through which she remembered. The memory of her parents' revulsion and her own revulsion at this ritual of sex was now set in a more complete perspective for Laura's safe retrieval of the original memory. It was at this point of the assessing stage that Laura experienced the greatest degree of tension. This tension was vital although for Laura it was very, very uncomfortable.

Intellectually she felt it important to recall and reframe her past in a way that did not continue the condemnation that kept her locked in an uncaring process. And yet as we began together to recall and reframe the past, Laura's resistance was very high. This resistance frustrated her, and so we turned our attention to it. Through her music and prayer, in and out of our sessions, Laura located the place in herself where the resistance was being "held." She began having serious cramps in her stomach and pain in her "womb." Through the coordinated sensitivity and attention of the campus chaplain, Laura's doctor, Laura, and myself, we assisted Laura in embracing the resistance and respecting the need for it. This embrace and respect for her resistance formed a new memory for Laura and an example of a ritual of care that empowered her to reconcile with her past as past. The resistance once understood and located worked with her instead of against her.

In our last month of the assessing process, Laura felt that she needed to find a way to process ritually the experience and memory of her forced abortion. She felt that she was more at peace with the times prior to and following the abortion. The abortion became an identified area from the past that needed to be contained in the present. The timing of this ritual in the therapeutic process was important. Laura knew that now was not the time, but she also knew the right time would come. To help prepare for this time, Laura concentrated on certain rituals in her present life that were important "as time markers while I figure out what I need to do." These time markers included frequent visits to the chapel on campus, work in a women's support group, volunteer work on refugee projects, and playing volleyball. These identified rituals from her present reality served as more than markers of time. They were stabilizing supports for Laura, grounding her in the present and offering her positive feedback about herself, her life, her intelligence, and her ability to be caring. These supports helped Laura to stay in the present as she prepared for the abortion ritual and her entrance into the next episode of therapy. Laura's movement from episode four to episode five was facilitated by her development of a word design chart (see figure 4).

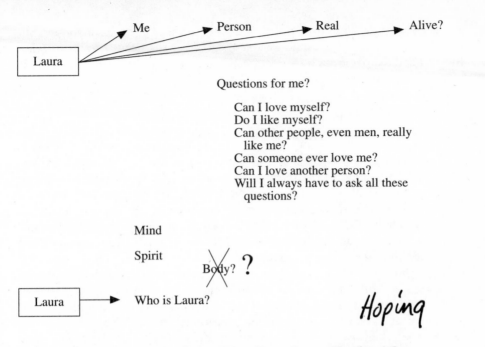

Figure 4. Laura's Chart of Herself as a Person Worthy of Care

As the chart indicates, Laura identified for herself an assignment: "To think about and feel *how* I can recognize *myself* as an important person about whom to care." At this time Laura was able to understand her body more clearly and found playing volleyball and jogging helpful occasions during which she could sense a connection between her body and mind. At the bottom of her diagram there is the word "hoping." When I asked Laura about this word, she described it as "being aware of being open to new hope."

Laura's words express a cautious optimism and a willingness to persevere. This perseverance relates directly to her approach to her own body, which is represented in her diagram as Body. Though Laura is understanding her body more clearly and engaging in activities that strengthen a positive connection between her body and mind, she is struggling with accepting and loving her body as a part of herself. The hope can be found in Laura's explanation of her diagram:

> Before I would have just left my body out of any description of me, or just have put an X over it. Now I have the word there and the question mark means that I am thinking and trying to feel something different. I don't know if I will ever love my body, but I don't want to punish it anymore. I have some hope and I am hoping too, I mean working on this.

Laura approached her next work in therapy with hope, a strong deliberateness, and a sense of growing trust not only in the process but more importantly in herself. She felt that she would be able to do what she needed to do to bring the past and its memories into a perspective that would not destroy her present or make her future impossible.

Episode 5. Bringing Strategies and Rituals Into the Therapeutic Context and Discovering Ways for Containing

For Laura the process of bringing in and recreating the strategies and rituals of her childhood in the therapeutic context was a fairly smooth one. She found a great deal of resolution in the identifying, naming, and assessing stages, and had already begun containing the strategies and rituals in the three dimensions of her childhood life: family, worship, and safer space. She now understood that even as a child her rituals in her safer space (her room) and the rituals and resources she was exposed to in worship and in church school themselves began the containment process for the destructive rituals of her family. Bringing these three dimensions and their rituals into our therapeutic context was something that Laura looked forward to and undertook easily. In this episode most of our time was spent on preparing Laura to address her teenage ritual of sex. Laura was understandably much more anxious about this ritual because it was the ritual that led to her pregnancy and ended with abortion.

Functionally, Laura had placed her life from thirteen through eighteen in a state of suspension. The most suspended part was her seventeenth year, during which she had become pregnant and had the abortion. Laura now recognized this entire period as being punctuated by the ritual of sex. The naming of this ritual helped raise memories to her conscious mind. However, the naming and the remembering did not provide in themselves a way to bring the ritual into the therapeutic space in order to contain it. Laura needed to plan some form of containment for this ritual. Coming to containment would mean coming out of suspension. This journey had to be carefully and caringly designed and executed. We spent time talking about this journey, and Laura prepared many charts for this time period. She found herself trusting more and more in this charting activity as her working strategy toward the journey. This in itself was important for Laura. It gave her a sense of partial control by involving her body and mind, and assisted her in reclaiming this time period in her life. Through her charts and word designs, Laura began to feel more comfortable with reclaiming her past. She felt safe enough to create an image by which she could imagine herself during her teenage years. In addition to her diagrams and designs, Laura began working with clay in an evening pottery class.

Laura found herself intrigued by the pottery process. She created seven pieces. These were pots of different forms and sizes. After creating the seventh pot, Laura came to realize that these pots were representations of her life during the teenage period. Through them Laura defined seven different phases of her life between thirteen and eighteen. Three of these pieces Laura associated with her life from thirteen to sixteen. One became a symbol for menstruation, another a symbol of the physical and psychological pain of development toward womanhood; the third symbolized her vagina. The fourth symbolized her first sexual encounter. The fifth pot symbolized Laura's pregnancy. She described it as "a form of a woman holding onto her belly with a form growing inside." The sixth pot contained two forms inside. Laura described these as "gravestones for me and my unborn child." The seventh pot also contained a form inside. The form was of a person who had a head, arms, legs, but only a shell of a torso. Laura described this as "my death following the abortion." She felt that her heart and her vulnerability were missing. She did not know where they were. Through these seven symbolic pieces and the blessing of them, Laura was able to visualize and touch her development during this painful part of her life. Each time she talked about one of these pieces, she would say a small prayer and sometimes would hum part of a hymn.

By the time we had gone through these seven symbolic pieces, Laura felt that she was ready to do something special with them. We devised a ritual in two parts for containing this period of her life. The first part took place in the therapeutic setting at the end of the fifteenth month. Laura planned a special program of music and brought in a portable keyboard. Through song and music we created an atmosphere and space for prayer over these seven symbolic pots. The prayer was for containment of this period in her life:

Jesus, give me the strength to put my past into these pots.
Let me try to let go of this but not bury it or lose it.
Help me to get rest from this, so I can move on with my life.
I love you, Jesus, please help me.

The second part of the ritual was directed toward finding her "lost body" after contacting her past. Laura asked if this ritual could take place outside of the therapeutic space with me present. We used an outdoor park, and Laura invited friends from the women's support group with whom she had shared her pottery and the story of her life. Prayer, singing, and telling stories of hope were included in this ritual. The group at one point surrounded Laura and each person touched her gently, inviting her to find her body again. Laura prayed for this also:

Jesus, I want to find my body again. Please help me find it and love it. Make it seem like a gift from God. It has been so, so long since I welcomed my body as a gift. Please help me with this.

Laura had another prayer service with the university chaplain the week following this ritual. Both the ritual and the prayer service enabled Laura to create a very strong link with her two communities: her community of friends and her church community.

Laura's pottery creations stayed in various locations. She sometimes left them with the chaplain, sometimes with certain women in the support group, and sometimes in the therapeutic space. Laura did not feel able to take them to her apartment. "They have too much energy just yet."

Episode 6. Developing Means for Creating New Memory, New Ritual

The last two months of therapy were devoted to episode six. During this time Laura was preparing to leave the university to begin graduate school. The process in this last episode with Laura was very much influenced by what had come before. Laura needed to talk about and understand the different dimensions of what had happened, what worked, and why. She was eager to begin graduate studies and eager to begin reconnecting with her body, but she was concerned also that in the move she would forget how to create strategies and use her music and charts. In light of Laura's impending move and her concerns, we addressed her anxiety by having her create a chart of the therapeutic journey (see figure 5).

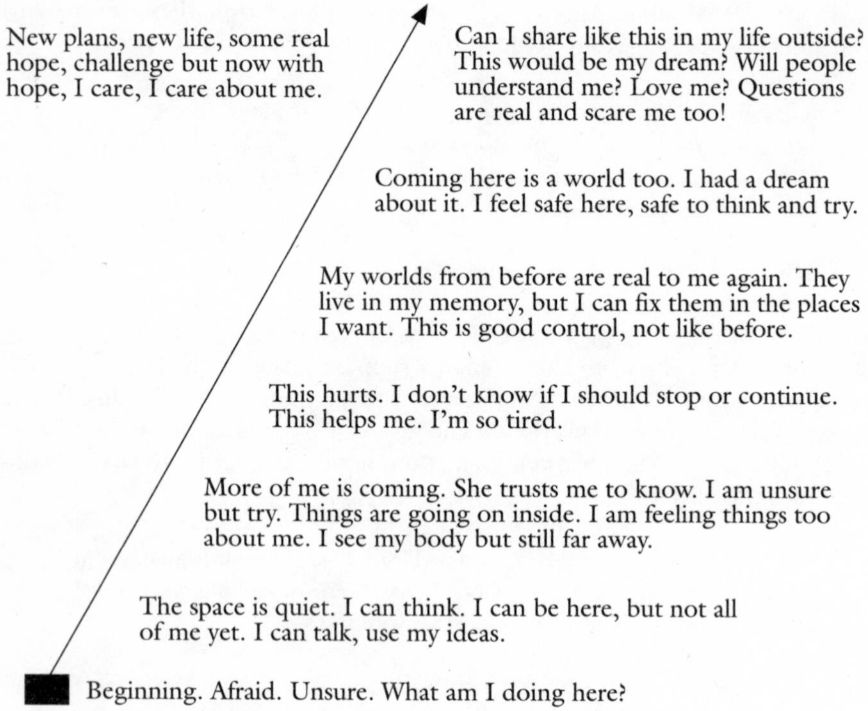

New plans, new life, some real hope, challenge but now with hope, I care, I care about me.

Can I share like this in my life outside? This would be my dream? Will people understand me? Love me? Questions are real and scare me too!

Coming here is a world too. I had a dream about it. I feel safe here, safe to think and try.

My worlds from before are real to me again. They live in my memory, but I can fix them in the places I want. This is good control, not like before.

This hurts. I don't know if I should stop or continue. This helps me. I'm so tired.

More of me is coming. She trusts me to know. I am unsure but try. Things are going on inside. I am feeling things too about me. I see my body but still far away.

The space is quiet. I can think. I can be here, but not all of me yet. I can talk, use my ideas.

Beginning. Afraid. Unsure. What am I doing here?

Figure 5. Laura's Chart of the Therapeutic Journey

Laura gained a new perspective through this chart. She could visualize our process and better understand all that had been done. Her anxiety decreased, and she was able to concentrate on what was yet to be done.

Laura felt that there was a very real piece of work still to do. Laura wanted to hold a prayer service for her aborted fetus. The planning of this event involved Laura, me, and the university chaplain. It was planned for a Saturday afternoon and involved a liturgy adapted from the Methodist tradition, including a number of hymns that Laura had chosen. It ended with her taking the pot containing the two symbolic gravestones and burying the pot in a space adjacent to the university chapel. The chaplain and I were the witnesses as Laura prepared the earth and buried the pot. It was a very powerful ritual for all of us. The impact of this experience upon Laura was quite evident.

Following this ritual, Laura and I spent our last month identifying several concerns she had in terms of continuing her worship life, prayer life, and hymn singing as she moved on to graduate school across the country. The fear Laura had was that through the process of moving she would need to keep redoing all of these rituals of containing. As we moved through the month and Laura tried to imagine herself in her new context, she was able to visualize the new memories formed over the past sixteen months. She began to trust that she would be able to recall the memory of these rituals and that their power would be sufficient to keep things contained. Once Laura felt somewhat calm about this, she raised another issue. She was concerned about her own sexuality and its being "dormant now for so many years." She wondered whether or not she would ever be able to be intimate with someone. At first Laura felt unsettled by this. But through prayer, reflection, and discussion, Laura embraced this wondering as itself a sign of change and growth. It signaled to her first, that she had come into the present; second, that she was becoming reacquainted with her body and its needs; and third, that she was desiring true intimacy that would not lead her away from her whole self. Laura began to trust that she had come a long way on her journey to intimacy and caring with herself. She believed now that this part of the journey would be the best guide to finding intimacy and caring with someone else. At our last session Laura brought with her a final design (see figure 6).

Laura understood her design as a sign of ending our process and beginning her future. Laura described our seventeen months as a "journey into myself and forward to God." Her final prayer was one of thanksgiving:

> God almighty and ever-present, thank you for your help here. Thank you for this relationship and for all my emotions, even the ones that still make me uncomfortable. Thank you for loving me and respecting me and guiding me and helping me guide myself out of hell and into the air and back into my body and soul.

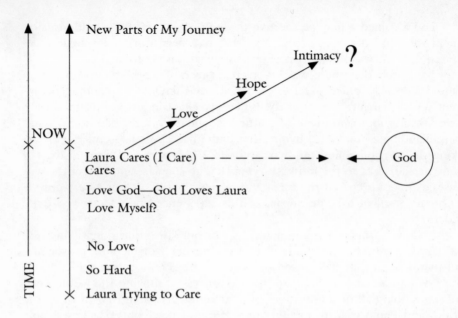

Figure 6. Laura's Hope for Intimacy and Caring with Self, God, and Others

CHAPTER 6

The Case of Anna: From Confession of Sin to Confession of Faith

I. Overview and Background

Anna, a Mexican-American woman, is thirty-three years old when we first meet. Pete, her husband, is a thirty-eight-year-old Euro-American. They have two children, Henry, age seven, and Maria, age four. Anna is living in a protective shelter with her children following an incident of abuse when Pete struck her. Anna has one other close relative, her mother, Theresa. Although the person in the therapeutic relationship is Anna, her situation in the family necessitates discussion of and points of interaction with Pete and her mother. These points will be presented as we move through the cycle of Critical Caring with Anna.

Family of Origin Information

Anna grew up in a tough neighborhood in a large inner city. She was a victim and survivor of childhood sexual abuse beginning at age ten at the hands of her stepfather, her mother's second husband. Theresa worked long hours to support Anna and herself after her second husband deserted both of them when Anna was fourteen. Theresa worked as a grocery clerk and had a second job as a seamstress. Her objective was to save enough money to move herself and Anna to a safer neighborhood not too far away. Theresa was able to accomplish this. When Anna turned fifteen, they moved to a new neighborhood.

Anna's mother did not know about the abuse that Anna had suffered.

The abuse happened infrequently. Anna, knowing how stressful her mother's life had been, working very long hours both during and after her marriages, decided not to tell her mother about it. Anna and her mother had never been close emotionally. Theresa did not realize that abuse was happening. She did notice that Anna became more quiet and more distracted between ten and fourteen. Yet since Anna's quietness was consistent with her personality from childhood, Theresa did not worry about it. Shortly after their move and the death of her stepfather, Anna told her mother what had happened. Theresa was very shocked and disturbed.

Theresa was not sure what to do with this information. She asked Anna if she wanted to visit the church. They were Roman Catholic, and there was a local church in their new neighborhood. Anna did not want to talk with any-one about this. Theresa also had experienced abuse from her second husband, physical abuse, and had not told anyone about it. She felt very sorrowful that this terrible thing had happened to her daughter. Anna and Theresa established a relationship as parishioners at the local Catholic church. In this different envi-ronment Anna was able to improve her work in high school. Following the third discussion with her mother about the abuse, she thought it best to "keep our past secret." From that time forward until many years later, Anna spoke to no one about the abuse, she felt that since Anna was doing well in school, everything was under control.

At eighteen, after finishing high school, Anna went to work as a clerk in a retail store. There she met Pete, who was working as a clerk and pursuing a degree in business at a local college. Anna and Pete fell in love and were mar-ried within fifteen months. Anna's mother was delighted by the relationship although she did not know Pete well. Theresa herself had been raised in a single-parent family by her mother. Theresa had never met her father. Theresa's first husband, Anna's father, deserted his family just after Anna's birth. There-fore Anna never got to know her own father. Theresa lived as a single parent until she married her second husband, Anna's stepfather, when Anna was nine. For Anna's mother, Pete represented a possibility for her daughter to move into a higher economic circle that would give Anna better financial se-curity and familial stability.

Pete had been raised in a lower-middle-class Irish and Italian neighbor-hood. Pete was the only child of an upwardly mobile family. Although the family itself had not moved beyond the upper realms of lower-class status, they dreamed that their only child, their only son, would do better. Pete's par-ents hoped that he would, according to Anna, "marry up or at least equal." This phrase made a deep impression on Anna when Pete's father told Anna this on her second visit to their home. His parents were not pleased with the relationship.

Pete, although coming from a different economic and cultural back-ground than Anna, had in some respects a very similar relationship to his family as Anna did to her mother. Pete was very quiet and contained at home. He did not feel close to his family. Pete, having always been, as he described himself to Anna, "an all-or-nothing kind of guy," decided to opt for Anna. He understood that this meant virtually severing ties with his family. Anna and Pete discussed this, and Anna was quite concerned. But she loved Pete and hoped his family would learn to accept her. Pete, in Anna's words, "expected me to appreciate his sacrifice and stand by him no matter what happened." Anna, therefore, described their marriage as "bringing about Pete's removal from his family and his clinging to me as his new family. This was a situation from which there was no turning back."

After marriage Anna remained in close contact with her mother but did so, in her words, "sneaking around Pete's schedule so he did not know how much I saw my mother." Pete wanted the family unit to be Anna and himself. He felt that since he had given up his family Anna should do the same and that she should want to do the same for the sake of their marriage. Anna agreed with her husband on the surface in order to avoid an argument. However, she felt that her own sanity and stability depended on a strong connection to her mother. Therefore, she continued to be very creative about the ways in which she maintained contact. Theresa understood, to some degree, Pete's concerns. Anna and her mother joined in a secret pact to continue their meetings.

The marriage seemed to be working well for a few years, and the couple was able to maintain a financial balance. Their first child, Henry, was born during the third year of the marriage. Anna stopped working and stayed home to care for Henry. At this point, however, she wanted to be openly close with her mother. She approached Pete about this, thinking that the baby would help to put things in a different perspective. She was surprised that he said, "No. And that's final." It appeared that he had no intention of "letting grandparents near our baby." Anna was somewhat surprised by this. She began to see a pattern developing toward their baby that she had felt toward herself: "That we were Pete's possessions, and he owned us, and he controlled us."

Anna was concerned about this and felt quite devastated. She again decided that she needed, on the surface, to obey Pete for the sake of the marriage. Things continued in this manner for the next three years, with Anna secretly visiting her mother's house whenever she could. Then Anna became pregnant unexpectedly and she gave birth to a little girl, Maria. Over the next year Anna became more and more distant from Pete. She continued to meet secretly with her mother. The more that Pete sensed this, although he did not know of their many meetings, the more he would overtly condemn Anna's need to see her mother. Anna drew further and further away from Pete and into herself.

After Maria's birth, Anna went through a postpartum depression. After a year of this undiagnosed condition, Anna felt that she needed to see her mother "to get back to myself" and to be open with Pete about this need. She felt that she must "confess to Pete the truth of my relationship with my mother." She was not sure why she had this need to confess except that she was so physically, psychologically, and spiritually debilitated that she knew she could not continue. She felt this might make things better. On the date she planned to tell Pete, she could not bring herself to say anything to him, afraid of what the consequences might be. Things continued in silence. Anna was less and less able to keep her life secret and began to feel more and more guilty about her sense of betraying her husband. Anna consciously decided to build different worlds for herself in her mind. This temporarily helped to contain the tension.

When Maria turned two, Anna began night college with Pete's support. Anna managed to isolate her world with Pete by focusing on school, the children, and their business plans. They had the idea of one day opening a retail shop of their own. Pete was doing well at work and was praised for his management abilities. The children seemed to be doing well although Anna noticed that both children seemed to be very, very sensitive to arguments between their parents. As Anna divided her worlds, things seemed more in control. An uncomfortable, yet somewhat stable silence existed now between Anna and Pete. The silence offered no outlet, no movement beyond itself.

Anna found a relief and release in her night-college classes. She looked forward to the two nights a week when she would be away from the house, away from Pete, away from the children, and gaining knowledge for the sake of their future. Through one of her friends in night school, Anna heard about an evening support group for incest survivors. Anna, after the birth of Maria, had begun thinking about the whole experience of incest that took place with her stepfather and began reading things about sexual abuse. Although she did not discuss it with anyone, it was on her mind. She had not told Pete about the incest with her stepfather. She decided not to tell Pete about the support group. She did tell him that she was joining a woman's group. Although he did not think it something necessary for her to do, he did not prohibit her from going.

This group gave Anna a sense of place and space in which she could talk about this part of her past with people who had gone through similar experiences. The group encouraged its members to keep a journal of thoughts, ideas, and memories that emerged. Anna wrote in her journal about being raped and physically abused by her stepfather and the need for secrecy through all of her life. Anna felt that at some time she would share her story with the women in the group. The group consisted of a variety of people from different racial and ethnic backgrounds. Anna felt comfortable in the group although she remained relatively quiet.

One evening while Anna was attending a group meeting, Pete was at home taking care of the children. Rummaging through the hall closet for one of the children's toys, he came across Anna's journal and began to read it. Pete had three responses, according to Anna:

> His first response was feeling anger and rage at my stepfather. Second, he felt anger at me for not telling him about this. And third, he felt disgusted at the thought of another man being "with his wife." He was

drinking heavily already, so by the time I got home Pete was drunk and very hyper. I noticed the journal on the kitchen floor with beer spilled all over it. I began to cry and started to run to the bathroom. Pete stopped me physically, stood in front of me, and smacked me across the face. I remember getting up and running to the bathroom, locking myself in, and staying in there all night.

The next morning Anna came out of the bathroom, checked on the children, and when Pete got up tried to talk to him. Pete would not talk. Anna was very concerned and very frightened. She later called her mother, and her mother advised her to stay calm, stay at home, not to talk about anything, and to get rid of the journal. For the next two weeks Pete continued drinking. On three different occasions he hit Anna, each time becoming more and more violent. During this period Pete did not speak to Anna except to communicate things in relation to the children or their schedule. Anna had bruises on her face, arms, and back. Finally she left for her mother's house. Her mother, who despite the second incident had advised Anna to wait, upon seeing the marks on Anna's face was convinced that Anna and the children should go to a shelter. Theresa felt they would not be safe at her house. Theresa brought Anna and the children to a nearby shelter recommended by the local church. Anna told her mother that she wanted to talk to a priest and needed to make her confession. Anna was very frightened, very concerned that she would lose her husband or would go back to him and live in fear of violence toward her and their children.

Pete, returning home from work that evening, realized that Anna and the children were gone. He called Theresa trying to locate them and to apologize. He told her that he wanted to find Anna and that he wanted things to get settled. He said that he did not know what he had done that was so wrong, but he wanted to have things "fixed up soon." Pete was surprised that Anna and the children were not at Theresa's house. Theresa told Pete that she did not know where Anna was.

Anna remained at the shelter for two months. The staff and counselors at the shelter helped Anna in several ways. Anna was very adamant about not wanting to have Pete arrested. Arrangements were made for Anna and the children to see Theresa. Anna also began to talk with counselors about what had happened. Through the activities of the shelter, Anna was able to make contact with a priest at the local church. He offered very supportive pastoral care, heard her confession, and talked with her about different kinds of support services and help through the parish. Anna was relieved at having that contact during this very turbulent part of her life. The future for Anna was unsettled, but she felt God was working with her. She was determined to find a way to get back with her husband for everyone's sake, especially for her children's. But she was not clear how this could be done.

She felt that she could work with the priest and through her faith to figure out what to do about her situation. She did not make contact with Pete for the first few weeks. After that, she called him but did not want to see him. He did not press her to see the children or to see her but indicated that he was sorry for whatever had happened and hoped that they could get back together. Anna said that she was not sure and that she needed some time and distance. A week later she called him and requested that he go to therapy, find some way to address his anger and rage, and that they try to find a person through whom they could communicate.

Over the next two weeks, in the second month of Anna's stay in the shelter, the priest became the mediator. Although Pete was initially resistant, he knew the situation was desperate, and he agreed to speak to the priest by phone. Anna felt some degree of safety and hope.

Toward the end of the second month Anna wanted to leave the shelter and move in with her mother. The children were experiencing some distress and disruption at the shelter, and Anna did not feel that Pete was a direct threat. At the end of the second month Anna moved into her mother's house with the children. The priest was working well as a mediator for Anna and Pete. Pete spoke to the priest several times during the second month of their separation. Pete reluctantly agreed to attend a men's therapy group for batterers. Pete's approach and his understanding of the need for therapy were very different from Anna's. He felt that he did not need therapy and that, although he regretted the violence toward his wife, he could contain and control the violence without intervention.

Anna felt strongly that Pete's word alone was not sufficient. Anna felt that she needed to be strong and decisive in relation to Pete's resistance to therapy. Although this was not a comfortable or familiar role for Anna, she knew that if there were not some sort of intervention, things would never change. Anna found the strength in herself with the help of advice from those at the shelter, the priest, and her mother to set certain conditions for herself and the children in relation to Pete. She wanted him to go to therapy and stop drinking. These were the conditions that Anna had set. Pete began attending the men's therapy group. It was at this point that Anna and I met for an initial session.

Religious Background

Anna grew up in a setting influenced by Roman Catholic teachings, church attendance, sacraments, and religious ritual. A group of women, including her mother, who were devoted to Our Lady of Guadalupe was also a strong influence on Anna. The group consisted of women with Mexican, Mexican-American, and similar backgrounds.

This strong female religious symbol, Our Lady of Guadalupe, made an impression on Anna from a very early age. This symbol and these women became a part of the worshiping community for Anna. Alongside traditional church attendance and the sacramental dimensions of church life, Anna held a special devotion to Our Lady of Guadalupe, which she and Theresa shared. On the whole, Anna's experiences in church were positive, and she found the time in worship nurturing. Even through the traumatic period of abuse between ten and fourteen, Anna found the worship experience a constant source of support. In her adult life, especially after her marriage to Pete who was also Roman Catholic, Anna did not attend church regularly. Contacting the priest when she entered the shelter brought Anna back to her need for these support systems and for their practical and symbolic strength. Anna and her mother renewed their devotional ritual to Our Lady at the same time as Anna began attending church again.

II. Moving Through the Episodes of Critical Caring

Therapeutic Timeline

My work with Anna extended over a thirteen-month period. Our work together sometimes included her mother, the children, the priest from the local church, and later Pete. A cultural consultant from the Mexican-American community became involved as well. During this thirteen-month period, Anna moved first from the shelter back to her mother's home and then, after a period of reconciliation, she and the children moved back together with Pete.

One of the issues that Anna and I dealt with was her choice, at this point in her life, to work with me and not a Mexican-American therapist. She voiced this choice clearly after our initial session: "Because of the relationship I am in, in a cross-cultural environment and with my children, I want to work a little outside of my own cultural community." Both of us felt comfortable working with one another. As we moved through the therapeutic cycle, we did draw at points on the services of a Mexican-American consultant. This assisted Anna in her search for ways of integrating her own background and culture into her decision-making process and her life with her children. Though I am a strong advocate of cross-cultural counseling and the value of working across cultures, I wondered whether Anna would be better suited to work with a female Mexican-American therapist. It was clear that she wanted to and needed to do her work with a woman. The freedom each of us felt to call upon a cultural consultant permitted both of us to feel comfortable with the decision to work together.

Anna and I discussed the therapeutic meeting schedule. In the beginning we met twice weekly. As she began to adjust to new living arrangements, we met once weekly. As need arose we met more or less frequently to suit the needs of Anna's changing situation.

Episode 1. Creation of Safe Therapeutic Space

The creation of a safe therapeutic space and a safe therapeutic relationship involved a two-month process with Anna. During our first session, Anna expressed her fear about trusting and yet her deep need and instinct to trust.

She was very eager to work on issues in pastoral therapy; yet she felt anxious at not knowing how to resolve all the issues. In light of events in Anna's past and present, she had every reason to fear the trusting process. In our first few sessions the issues of trust and the need to suspend trust became important ones for Anna. In her words, "It helps to feel okay about not trusting everyone. I mean I have to figure out how to trust and not trust."

These words let her express some fears and anxieties about being in therapy in terms of her own past experiences. Anna had worked very hard to build an internal system of different worlds. She was afraid of exploring her past despite the fact that she felt the need to do so. Anna wanted to find a way to move forward with her life for the sake of her children and for herself. However, therapy seemed "a little scary too." When Anna voiced this fear, she was able to understand and later to let go of it. Feeling the freedom to ask questions and to design her own work in therapy gave Anna a sense of control. This helped her to begin trusting our process.

Anna wanted to be able to think about therapy as safe space. At this point, especially during the first month, Anna was exhausted and unable to focus her full attention, which was extremely frustrating for her. She wanted to move forward, but the more she tried the more frustrated she became. I asked Anna if she had any hobbies or things that she did to relax. She said that she had always liked writing poems, keeping her journal, and sewing. Anna brought in a few samples of her poetry and her fabric creations. The physical presence of these things seemed to help her relax. In our third session Anna asked if we could pray over the poems and the pieces of fabric. She wanted to "carry the prayer with me when I leave here." We did pray. This experience of prayer became one of the grounding points for the therapeutic process. It helped to create a safe therapeutic space and a peace that surrounded Anna. During this period when we were creating a safe space, Anna became more and more calm and able to talk about her beliefs, "the three parts of my trinity:" "First, there's God, I mean the Father, up in heaven and kind of removed; then there's Jesus, present but not always so close; and then there's Our Lady of Guadalupe, who is the closest to me, like a mother, and sometimes like a friend."

The three members of Anna's trinity became an important resource for the therapeutic process. In some ways they symbolized Anna's life journey. Our Lady of Guadalupe symbolized a way for Anna to deal with her suffering and pain. Our Lady functioned for Anna as a mothering and nurturing dimension of herself. The symbol of God the Father was the most inaccessible. However, she gave to God the Father "the part of me I can't look at yet." So this symbol became Anna's conscious holding zone. Jesus was more accessible and served as "my link to my pain, not to forget it."

Anna brought in a small statue of Our Lady of Guadalupe in the fifth session. At first she was hesitant to take it out of her bag. When I asked her if she was afraid, she said, "No, I'm not afraid, but she is so special, and I want her to have a place here." I asked Anna how we could create a space for Our

Lady, and she said, "Well, someplace nice and safe and loving." Those words described not only a place for the statue but also what Anna was yearning for in her own life and relationships. We found such a place on a stand in the corner of the room. Anna brought the statue back and forth to therapy with her. Sometimes she would keep it in her bag; at other times she would take it out to have it visibly present with us. The image of Anna's trinity was quite useful in our sessions. Through the different symbols, Anna was able to raise questions about authority, companionship, mothering, and nurturing.

By the end of our second month of work, Anna and the children were adjusting to arrangements at her mother's house. Pete remained in the place where they had been living. He had begun therapy in relation to anger control. He saw very little of Anna, but he did have visits with the children. These seemed to be working well. Anna's mother, Theresa, encouraged Anna to stay with her. Anna herself was surprised by her mother's response. She found it supportive that her mother did not push her back into the marriage with Pete at this point. Anna, however, considered herself to be married, to be Pete's wife. She wanted, as she said, "to have time and calmness for us to try to work things out."

Episode 2. Entry Into Symbolic Reality

Anna's movement through the second episode took place over a one-month period involving six sessions. However, it was complicated by the fact that Anna was in transition. In terms of Anna's understanding of her present symbolic reality, there did not seem to be many grounding points for her. However, even in the midst of transition and tension, Anna was able to name her present primary resource as her faith, particularly expressed through the presence of Our Lady of Guadalupe. Her children were a source of stabilization but also of worry. Her mother and her small group of friends from night school were also resources. Anna described these resources as "real but floating in and out of my worlds."

Anna was able to identify four different "worlds" that we needed to explore if we were going to understand the symbolic reality that had shaped her and was shaping her. Gaining entry into these worlds was facilitated by her use of the resources that she had come to depend on: her poetry and her fabric creations. Anna was able to create a collage of words and fabric that helped us begin. The collage mapped her symbolic reality in the following way: She identified the world of her childhood through the words "silence, faith, and terror." She categorized her next world as her late-teenage–young-adulthood years and described it as "a little hope and more safety." Anna marked the beginning of this world when she moved with her mother to the new neighborhood. The third world for her was her marriage to Pete and her children. She captured this world with the terms "love, trust, and new life." Anna's fourth world, her present, was represented by the words "separation, mistrust, and fear."

When Anna presented and talked about her collage in therapy, she became almost silent when she came to her fourth world. She said finally, "The present is not the end of my worlds, but it is a frightening place to be." I asked Anna where her faith was in each of these worlds. She said: "Through all of these my faith has a very important part in each world. It helped me live through different experiences. I don't know how faith is going to help me move to the future, but I only know it's a big part of my present." During this month Anna found it helpful to continue her sewing projects. One thing Anna knew about her present world was that she desperately needed to have things to hold onto as she was "outside of my real home and not knowing if it will be home again." In addition to these sewing projects, Anna continued to work on her journal and poetry. These very concrete activities in conjunction with her prayer life helped to keep Anna in balance during this difficult period of transition.

Episode 3. Identifying Central Strategies and Rituals of Symbolic Reality

Working through episode three took us two months. Having identified her worlds, Anna was able to approach the strategies and rituals that emerged for her out of each world. The world of childhood for her was one split between "the memories of terror and silence, and the memories of faith." Terror and silence and the rituals around them took place both inside her world of home and outside in the neighborhood. The abuse and its resulting anxiety left Anna feeling that she had nowhere to go. She recalled creating her own rituals as a child, trying "to cleanse myself and take the fear and put it somewhere else."

Anna found some comfort in her faith. Her silence and terror could be shared with Our Lady of Guadalupe. She did this largely in silence, but sometimes in vocal prayer as well. The same statue that Anna brought into the therapeutic space was what she clung to as a child after she had been terrorized or when she felt very frightened. Her faith, represented through this object, provided a ritual of survival in her first world. Anna's next world, her teens and young adulthood, took her geographically to another location. Anna remembered this move as being something more than just physical. It represented a move toward greater safety. Anna expressed this period in her life as being one "in which I felt more freedom, especially in the development of my faith." She recalled being able to create in the privacy of her own room her own prayer schedule and devotional time. In this world she began making friends and slowly feeling the weight of abuse lifted, especially after the death of her stepfather.

It was in Anna's third world, that of her marriage to Pete and the world of their family, that Anna remembered trust and love emerging for the very first time in her life. At first she felt very safe with Pete and experienced a freedom to explore "a new world and a new way of understanding things." In retrospect, however, Anna remembered that it was in the beginning of the marriage that she felt the most distance from her central symbol, Our Lady of Guadalupe. She did not know how to share this in her marriage, so she distanced herself from it. Anna continued to attend church but felt uncomfortable with her home devotional ritual. This was the one part of her life, a very important part, that she did not hold in common with her husband.

As the marriage continued, Anna discovered that she needed her devotional ritual in order to keep her past and present in balance. Therefore, Anna retreated more and more into the symbolic world of her past. The patterns of secrecy and silence returned for her in an uncomfortable way. These became manifest especially after the birth of her first child when she found it necessary to return secretly to her mother's house to reclaim rituals of her past. Anna felt herself becoming more and more separated from Pete. Pete felt threatened by Anna's symbols, her past, her connection to her mother and to the world they represented. This caused a tension in Anna that aggravated her past unresolved memories of silence and terror.

The way in which Anna was able to survive this period was to consciously construct a divided life. She had become quite adept at this survival skill in her childhood. She therefore resurrected this pattern. But Anna did not want to hide the way she made meaning out of her culture and experience. As an adult this survival pattern of silence and secrecy became more and more problematic. At night after everyone else was sleeping, Anna would go into the kitchen, light a candle, and find her statue of Our Lady of Guadalupe, which she kept hidden. She would then have her special prayer ritual. She described this ritual as being "the way to keep my feet on the ground without footprints." This ritual of secrecy was a mode of survival for Anna. The nightly rituals kept her spiritually contained but caused her to live in psychological terror that Pete would find out and disapprove.

Her fourth world, the world of her present, began for Anna when Pete discovered her journal and became violent toward her. Anna felt this world would be temporary, but its length was an unknown. What helped Anna through this time was a nightly ritual, done after the children had gone to sleep, done sometimes alone and sometimes with her mother. It was a ritual of devotion to Our Lady of Guadalupe. Although this period in Anna's life was filled with tension, "as though my feet are not on the ground," it also contained the hope of liberation for her. This liberation stemmed from her conviction that, for the sake of her children and for herself, she could not be imprisoned anymore by violence. This conviction came to life through her prayers. Anna prayed for her life to change, not just for the ability to survive or endure.

> Mother in Heaven, please help me to get a better life for my children. Don't let them suffer. I want them to have hope and happiness. Help me to know what to do now with Pete, with everything.

Toward the end of this two-month segment, Anna talked more and more about the beneficial aspects of her working with the priest in the parish who was very supportive of her. She wanted to know if the priest could be invited to one of our sessions to give a blessing on our process. Anna felt that she needed to have our work blessed to strengthen it and also to celebrate her growth in faith. Anna no longer believed that the suffering in her life was due to her lack of faith or her sin. The priest and I welcomed this joint meeting. At the end of one session, the priest visited with us. In preparation for this visit Anna brought in candles, her statue of Our Lady of Guadalupe, and various fabric creations and poems that represented her four different worlds. The blessing and prayer session lasted only ten minutes. However, the effect of it on Anna was beyond measure. It offered her a very important new memory of hope. Anna was later to mark this session as the beginning of a new world.

Episode 4. Assessing the Impact of Strategies and Rituals on the Caring Process

As we began episode four, the assessing process, we were moving into month six of our work together. Anna remained with her mother, and this arrangement was working fairly well. She had resumed evening classes, working toward a business degree. She and Pete had met a few times with the priest, and Pete verified for Anna that he had been attending a therapy group for men who have been physically abusive. Anna felt this was a positive sign from Pete that he recognized a problem and was trying to address it constructively. Anna, through her return to night-school classes, continued with the women's support group. The children at this point also seemed to be adjusting relatively well to the environment with their grandmother. They continued to see their father on a regular basis. This was a relatively calm period in Anna's life. With these stabilizing activities as background, Anna experienced a freeing of some of her energy to be able to look at strategies and rituals of her past and to assess their impact on how she understood caring.

Assessing the impact of strategies and rituals on Anna's caring process took place over a three-month period. Anna already had begun to feel the impact of these strategies and rituals in her past and in the work we had done in terms of identifying and naming her strategies, rituals, and her four worlds. The rhythm that was happening in her own world now marked for Anna an emerging fifth world. She named this fifth world "My World of Faith." Understanding what this meant to Anna is important for what happened during this stage, the assessing stage. In naming this stage "My World of Faith," Anna was identifying a caring process that was happening inside herself. Key to this process was her unwillingness to continue to live imprisoned by terror or fear. Her situation, at this point, had not changed dramatically. She was still in a period of separation from her husband, still in a temporary living situation with her mother, and still concerned about the future for her children. The externals had not varied. What was different for Anna was the change internally, her inner perspective. Being able to name her unwillingness to have her children and herself imprisoned by terror and fear and the strength gained through her strategies and rituals had given Anna a perspective from which to assess her past. By naming this time in her life as a new world, her fifth world, Anna was symbolically and literally creating a new vantage point. She described this fifth world in this way: "This is my world of faith, of hope for my children and tomorrow."

She chose this name based on a sermon that examined the move from sin to grace, the restoring of relationship to God, and the offer of a new proclamation, a new confessing of faith. Anna found the confessing of faith to be healing. It gave her distance from the imposing framework of labeling her life as the confessing of sin. "For the sake of my children," Anna said, "I want them to have a pass-down of faith and not sin. I can see sin in a new way. It's not what I thought for so long."

This vantage point of faith created a perspective that gave her strength, stability, and a way of connecting with her past. She was excited about looking again at the past to decipher what had given her strength and what had taken strength away from her. As Anna entered this fifth world, she knew she was ready to do the assessing process. This knowledge came through Anna's trusting that there was life beyond the four worlds, beyond the chaos, terror, and forced silence. When she trusted this and had evidence for trusting it, she found strength in herself and a way to ask for help that grew out of that strength.

We spent the first part of the assessing process examining the strategies and rituals of Anna's four worlds, first uncovering the theme of hope that ran through them. That theme was her faith, especially and consistently nurtured through her evolving relationship with Our Lady of Guadalupe. Identifying this theme gave Anna courage to analyze her past and to realize that she had survived what she had lived through in her past. Anna had not understood this before as survival nor had she been able to appreciate her own strength that had kept her alive. Along with arriving at and naming her fifth world, isolating and identifying this theme of strength also helped Anna to gain the courage to look at the strategies and rituals that deeply wounded her.

The most severely wounding rituals began at the point in her childhood when Anna was physically and sexually abused by her stepfather. Anna was now able to recall some of these memories clearly. The means she developed to move from memory recall to assessment was an impressive process. Anna, after having prayed for guidance from Our Lady, realized that she needed to visualize and touch her assessment process. In her words, "I know now that my sewing and poetry are a part of me. They really have a meaning, so I need them to do this."

Anna's poetry and sewing helped her assess the ritual's impact on caring in each of her four worlds. In world one, that of childhood and the rituals of silence and terror, Anna visualized the impact as the loss of her voice and as the loss of her body. She created a collage to illustrate this. The poem that accompanied the collage was the following:

> Once there was me, a child whole.
> Later I could not cry, no sound would come.
> When my eyes looked down there was no body.
> Only pain, only pain.

In the second world, her later teens and early adulthood, the impact was a loss of her mind. Anna described that loss as being forced by the patterns of secrecy and silence. However, Anna felt that she had held onto her soul. Her poem for this world's assessment was:

> He made me keep silent.
> Even after he was dead
> I couldn't speak.
> Even in my mind a place
> went dead.
> Not even the pain lived there.
> But my soul lived still.
> It still lived.

As she moved into assessing her third world, that of marriage, she felt at first that her soul had come to life. But as the marriage developed, and she was forced to abandon her positive resources or later to hide them, the strength turned into yet another loss, that of her culture and heritage. During her life in world three, Anna was bearing children and putting forth new life into the universe. Yet she also felt her life was being taken away from her. Her poem for this world read:

> Why God is there all this pain?
> I give birth to my babies and want
>   to give to them.
> But inside I hide, I hide again from them.

The impact of her fourth world, the world of separation and transition, Anna described as horrifying and strengthening. Her poem for this world's impact was:

> No home, no home.
> No home inside or out.
> Pain and bruises inside and out.
> Where do I go from here?
> Why is my sin so great?

Maybe not sin. I confess faith.
I am a child of God.
How can I feel hope inside?
I do.
I hope.
I confess faith.
God, Our Lady, Jesus help me—
Help my faith.

From her perspective of the fifth world, the world of faith, Anna found the strength to name the strong theme of loss that carried her through assessment of each of these four worlds. Anna was stunned and overwhelmed at the impact of her great losses: her voice, her body, her mind, her culture, and her heritage. There was nothing left to lose unless it was life itself. It was at this point, after the assessment process, that Anna talked about her decision to leave Pete and move to the shelter in a way that she had not talked about or reflected upon it before. Anna had thought of committing suicide, but her choice for the shelter was, in retrospect, a choice for life. Even in the midst of all that happened and that was happening, Anna never doubted the presence and love of God and of Our Lady of Guadalupe.

Coming full circle to her present world, Anna was struggling with a way to reclaim the resources of her culture. Deep inside, assessing the journey through her life led Anna to realize how much she wanted to keep her marriage but not without respect and caring. This created a great source of tension within Anna. Anna now was experiencing the need to make a connection with a Mexican-American consultant in order to sort through how to bring the resources of her culture and work into her cross-culture situation. I provided Anna with a short list of resources. She did not call any immediately. However, Anna seemed relieved that she now had a piece of paper with phone numbers on it of women from within her own culture who could talk with her about her struggles.

As we moved through the three months of the assessing process, Anna began to journal more intensely and to remember more and more particular memories. Anna became more comfortable in her woman's group and felt that she wanted to share a bit of our therapeutic process with this safe group. Anna found the experience of sharing very liberating. Anna felt she had something to contribute to these other women who had gone through experiences of incest and abuse and had found their own ways of survival.

At the end of this three-month period, Anna had made phone contact with a cultural consultant and was planning to visit with her. Making this contact was a significant act for Anna on the symbolic as well as the literal levels. She was trying in all aspects of her life—in relation to her mother, in relation to her children, in relation to what might come about with Pete, and in terms of her own culture—to approach each with the best sense of Critical Caring, trying to find out what to salvage, and how to scavenge responsibly. Anna continued to meet with the priest and to talk with him about a variety of issues. Anna found her resource network growing and felt it was time to strategize how to move forward.

Episode 5. Bringing Strategies and Rituals Into the Therapeutic Context and Discovering Ways for Containing

At the very beginning of our therapeutic process Anna and I examined the model of Critical Caring. Anna was intrigued by episode five. She said, "I even had a dream about this, and if I ever survive to get there, I will celebrate." Anna and I did celebrate her arrival at episode five. We prepared a special feast that we enjoyed during one of our sessions. This feast symbolized our hard work and Anna's progress. Anna already had brought the positive strategies and rituals of her faith and of her relationship with Our Lady of Guadalupe into the therapeutic space. But the rituals of wounding that had created such terrifying memories were different. These threatened Anna and caused great apprehension. Anna's apprehension was real and was respected. Only a knowledge of safety and security in her present perspective would responsibly address Anna's apprehensions. When she felt these were in place, she knew that these past rituals could be contained, though she remained anxious about how this would happen.

Anna became very involved in this containing process and was determined that we move in chronological order and in stages. She saw things in a chronological way, as her worlds' approach indicated. We spent three months working on containing her past rituals and memories. It is important to indicate what was happening in Anna's life in order to understand how and why we worked as we did. Anna had begun to see Pete on a somewhat regular basis. She very much wanted the family to stay together. The children wanted to be reunited with their father as well, but Anna wanted to wait a bit longer for this. Anna asked if it would be possible for Pete to come to one of our sessions and be part of this stage of our process. I concurred. She had discussed this with her priest, with Pete, and with her cultural consultant. All seemed to be supportive of this idea. If Anna was going to be reunited with Pete, it would have to be done in a way that helped both members of the couple to feel as safe, secure, and responsible as possible. Therefore, during this three-month period we invited Pete to join us in different ways. We set up a meeting at which Pete, the priest, Anna, and I met. At this meeting Anna shared what she felt she needed in terms of moving through her past and finding strength to move ahead in the marriage and with their family. The invitation to Pete was sometimes to listen and observe. At other times Pete and Anna came to discuss and plan rituals for her past. At one session the priest came to bless the process and all of us.

At the first of these sessions, Pete was very tense and yet nonresistant. It was clear that he had been doing work in the context of his therapy group and that he was very sorry for having struck his wife. It was also obvious that he was a person whose culture and personality did not approach reality in the same way as Anna did. Anna's concerns were that she be free to be who she was and not to deny the different parts of herself in her relationship with Pete. When she was able to talk about what she wanted, how she felt, and what she needed to move forward, Pete began to understand better Anna's painful past and its patterns of abuse, silence, and secrecy.

One of the most powerful sessions took place with Pete and the priest. Anna wanted to have a healing ritual around the night when Pete struck her. Anna and Pete had met to work on this ritual. In the session with all of us present, Pete began this healing ritual by making a very strong confession of his sin against Anna: "I have sinned against you by hitting you and by not understanding you or letting you understand me." After these words, Anna said a prayer with tears running down her face. The space became silent. At our next session Anna said, "When Pete confessed to me, at that moment I really felt we could have a new beginning."

It was also at that moment that Anna believed she could allow Pete into her fifth world, the world of faith. Anna and I engaged in a number of different containment attempts for the wounding rituals of her past and present. Each of these involved a ritual of blessing. Anna's priest was present for two of these rituals. By the time we had worked our way through her life's rituals, Anna had gained a great deal of strength through these healing and containing services. She went back to the ritual of abuse with her stepfather after we had come full circle into her present.

On this return we planned a special healing ritual and invited the priest, Pete, and also Anna's mother. The presence of Anna's mother and Pete was very important for Anna. Anna said the prayers at the beginning. She had created a special fabric container into which she would place her memories of abuse. At the end of the ritual we held hands in a circle, and everyone was invited to pray. We each prayed, but Anna remained silent. Then as we stood in the circle, Anna announced in a low but calm voice that she had found her voice again. Through the rituals that had preceded this one, Anna had begun to contain her memories to the point where she found a way of reclaiming her culture, her heritage, her mind, her body, and finally, now, her voice. The presence and cooperation of her mother and Pete throughout this process symbolized for Anna a concrete hope for a new beginning in her relationship with Pete.

Episode 6. Developing Means
for Creating New Memory, New Ritual

As we entered the sixth episode, Anna and I had been working together for eleven months. As with each of the other episodes, things shifted or changed for Anna's situation externally and internally. Following the three months of work on the healing and containing of the rituals of her past, Anna and the children felt able to move back into the same household with Pete. One of the new rituals, therefore, that took place at the very beginning of the twelfth month of time together was a ritual for blessing of the family. This took place with Anna, Pete, the priest, and myself in their home. The priest performed a ritual of blessing on the house and on the relationship in which we all took part. Toward the end of this ritual, as had been planned, Anna's mother, Theresa, came with the children, and we had a celebration for a new beginning. This very concrete ritual of reentry for Anna, Pete, and the children set the pace for the work of creating new memory and new rituals in our last episode, our last two months of work.

Over this two-month period Anna continued to meet with the priest and her women's group. She wanted to stay with the themes of entry and reentry for her life, just as the ritual of blessing had done with her home. Anna wondered how her return home would affect her relationship with Our Lady of Guadalupe. Anna took great care to strengthen this relationship. She was very deliberate in her journal writing, in her praying, and in her creating process through her sewing. Anna found that her relationship with Our Lady remained central to her life. Her sustaining prayer ritual with Our Lady of Guadalupe, the ritual of constancy throughout her past, now inspired Anna to move beyond survival to love and respect for herself. Though we worked on other strategies and rituals, this one was the positive foundation for all the others.

At the end of our time together, Anna told me that she was working on a fabric creation for me. She told me that it would take a while for it to be completed but brought with her a working sketch of what it would look like. Anna had worked to envision and create a different world for herself, for her children, and with Pete. This was Anna's closing prayer in our final session:

> Our Lady, bless this lady who has helped me so much. She understands who I was and let me show her who you were. Give us strength to go our own ways and your blessings today and for our children's tomorrows.

CHAPTER 7

The Case of Beth and Gina: When Theology Creates a Context for Terror

Opening Case Note: At the end of Part I five reasons were given for the choice of cases selected. The fourth reason, the pastoral and clinical challenge of the case for my development as pastoral psychotherapist, must be underscored as we approach the case of Beth and Gina. Though each of the preceding cases has raised vital concerns for understanding Critical Caring and for undertaking the theological challenges involved, the following case has accomplished this at every level. The relational context of the couple, that of being in a homosexual partnership, though not the individuals themselves, brought me as pastoral psychotherapist into direct confrontation with denominational teachings, theological and dogmatic, concerning homosexuality. Before my work with this case I had been active and vocal concerning my denominational disagreement from pastoral, theological, and clinical perspectives. However, I had not fully understood or named the consequences of this theological inheritance as theological terror.

Through my work in this case the pastoral, theological, and clinical challenges emerged through a process that I had not quite anticipated. When such happens, the pastoral psychotherapist is in a critical situation. Critical Caring is vitally needed so that the necessary degrees of both distance and engagement can be maintained. In the course of the case presentation, and as appropriate to it, material is included on this process as dimensions of it were consciously brought into the therapeutic context. Naturally, this was done cautiously,

121

carefully, and in coordination with recommendations from my professional colleagues involved in case review and familiar with the clinical approach being used.

I. Overview and Background

Beth and Gina come for counseling together, as a couple. Beth is an English-American woman, age thirty-one. Gina is a Mexican-American woman, age twenty-nine. Beth and Gina have been in a committed relationship for three years. Both are professional women. Beth works as a buyer of woman's wear for a large international corporation. Gina is a graphic artist. They met years earlier in undergraduate school at a large university on the East Coast. They were friends for several years when both lived in Europe, Beth in England and Gina in France.

Beth and Gina were both raised in Christian contexts. Gina's background is Roman Catholic; Beth's background is Presbyterian and Congregational. Both women have been and continue to be deeply religious and spiritual, and to a greater or lesser degree each has maintained contact with the denomination of her past. Beth and Gina have come to pastoral psychotherapy because they have identified two issues with which they are struggling.

First, both desire to have their relationship recognized and blessed by the Christian church. Ceremony and ritual are very important to each of the women and are important to them as a couple. Though they have had a celebration with friends at their own covenant ceremony three years ago, they each in different ways express the desire for a blessing "by God in a public celebration."

The second issue concerns the nature and extent to which the world, outside of their friends, is responding to their commitment to each other. Whereas Gina is in a work environment in which she has many acquaintances who know about and support her relationship with Beth, Beth has found her work environment to be stifling in regard to her relationship to Gina. Beth is welcomed at Gina's workplace, but the reverse is not true. Beth has heard crude jokes by her colleagues concerning "butches and fags." She is convinced that her work environment is not a safe place in which to share the deep feelings of her personal life because she is in love with another woman instead of a man. Gina finds it difficult to understand and appreciate the consequences of spending ten hours a day in Beth's type of work environment.

These two identified issues are significant for Beth and Gina as they come to therapy. They are issues that challenge the living of life as a Critical Caring process and involve both the practical and the symbolic levels. We find two women in a committed and covenanted relationship who are struggling with issues of self-acceptance and other-acceptance of their committed relationship. Since the work contexts for Beth and Gina are different, this has ramifications at both the practical and symbolic levels. We are dealing with a complex situation of concern for the relationship and concern for the different personal and work worlds in which Beth and Gina function.

Family of Origin Information

Gina is not now close to her family of origin, which consisted of mother, father, maternal grandmother, two older sisters, and a younger brother. One of her older sisters knows about her relationship with Beth and is somewhat supportive. Gina's mother is now deceased, and her father is ill. Her father has told her, "Live your life as you have to, but I don't want to hear about your having relations with a woman."

Beth's family of origin, consisting of mother, father, and older brother, has virtually dismissed her. She quotes her mother as saying, "Until or unless you live decently, I don't accept you as my daughter." Beth's father wrote a note to her that read:

> How could you have done this to us? Whose fault is this? I am sickened by this! I can't get over all this. Your mother and I are very worried and somewhat angry. Please don't call us. If we need to, we'll call you or meet you away from your apartment.

The relationship between Gina and Beth has presented a situation to both their families that they had not encountered before. Both families have found it difficult to know what to do with this kind of relationship and have actively shunned their child. Ideas, images, value systems, and dimensions of culture have come into conflict. The families' worldviews allow no room for this kind of committed relationship between women. Both Gina and Beth, when discussing family, have commented that although they have families of origin they do not consider them to be "family." Both have made efforts to find "a new family" comprised of friends and acquaintances who support their being in relationship together or who do not find the relationship in itself to be a stumbling block. When Gina and Beth talk about their present family, they refer to a group of supporting friends whom they have in common and also to the friends each has individually as well. Each has a "family of friends" individually, and they have a "family of friends" in common.

Prior to their involvement with each other, which for each woman was the first significant experience in a woman-woman relationship, each had been in short-term relationships with men. Both report that, before their emerging love relationship, each had an existing but strained relationship with her family of origin. Gina's family offers, even at this point, a bit more support for the relationship, though culturally her father and her brother actively view it as a violation of community, family, and morality. Beth describes the experience with her family prior to this relationship as "distantly friendly." Beth views her family as by nature and by culture primarily British, which in her analysis means "very reserved and categorical about the proper actions one should pursue." Beth's family has viewed this relationship as culturally and familially outside the realm of what is acceptable or what is possible.

Though coming from different cultural and familial backgrounds, each woman has met with similar responses that have eliminated for each certain resources they had looked to in the past for emotional and personal support. Both Gina and Beth had anticipated some alienation from their families at first, but neither perceived that it would remain for so long with so little hope for change. Both Gina and Beth in their different ways talk about this loss of family as significant. Each has done some grieving over the loss, but neither has completely grieved for the loss of their families. Each maintains some faint hope for relationship with their families or certain family members again in the future.

Faith and Spiritual Life Concerns

Both Gina and Beth note how much their faith and spiritual life mean to them. Faith was a resource for them as children and as they were growing up in their different familial and cultural contexts. Gina and Beth also express how much their faith and spiritual life mean to them in the present and, to use Beth's words, "I know my faith can help me face the truth about my sexuality and personhood." Both women are experiencing the very real and agonizing irony that the religious institutions which have given them support and hope also have particular beliefs which cause them to live in theological terror, to doubt the love and the care of God for them. With tears, Gina said:

> My God, God help me through all this. Those nights I thought of ending it all, God was with me. I know this. But the mask of God, the church, talks about damnation for "women like me" and makes me question whether there is a God, or if God is real, at least the God who got me through all this.

Beth's words are more stark: "It's illogical. God can't be both A and negative A. If God loves me, God loves me as I am." These assessments of the complicated and ironic positioning of God's care, denominational belief structures, and their own spirituality present an important part of the picture for understanding Gina's and Beth's philosophical and theological orientations at the beginning of the therapeutic process.

Both have different images of God as they come to therapy. Gina's image is of God "in relationship," and Beth's image is of God as "the abstract foundation." Though each has a different image of God, their desire to relate to God and the consequences of their present context on that relationship are similar. Gina currently feels unable to reach toward God as the separation in her drawing line indicates (see figure 7).

Beth's image of her relationship to God involves a conception of God as the life force. Beth feels her crossing out of the circle in her drawing shows that she cannot obtain access to this foundation, this life force (see figure 8). Though their images of God are quite different, the consequences of the struggles they are pursuing are very similar. Gina and Beth seek pastoral therapy specifically because, in Gina's words, "we need to find a way through this, and not just to understand this." The way through for them means struggling

Figure 7. Gina's Image of Her Relationship to God

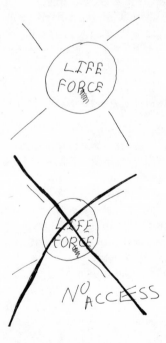

Figure 8. Beth's Image of Her Relationship to God

beyond the point of understanding to a resolution that includes facing the theological dimension of their lives, both individually and together.

II. Moving Through the Episodes of Critical Caring

Therapeutic Timeline

The therapeutic relationship with Gina and Beth took place over a period of nineteen months. During this time we arrived mutually at a plan for the sessions. This included a pattern of flexibility that appeared to match the needs presented and to allow for progress through the various issues that arose. For the major part of our time all three of us met together. However, scattered throughout the nineteen-month period there were times when I met in individual sessions with Gina and Beth. This kind of pattern might not make sense as a rhythm when working with other couples. However, in this instance both Gina and Beth thought it important that as they worked together on issues of concern in their relationship they also needed to work individually on specific issues. This idea was discussed, and we collaboratively decided that such flexibility was a pattern that made sense in terms of the overall goals of therapy. The nineteen months of therapy, therefore, were focused on a movement through the therapeutic episodes at three different levels: Gina's and Beth's movement through the stages together as a couple, Gina's individual movement through the stages, and Beth's individual movement through the stages. Both Gina and Beth came to the therapeutic relationship with a sense of balance and ability, as Gina described it, "to jump into the therapeutic process." Both seemed equally ready to do this, which facilitated the therapeutic process.

Episode 1. Creation of Safe Therapeutic Space

The first month of the therapeutic process was devoted to creating a safe space for Gina and Beth. This creation involved their willingness to bring in objects that had symbolic significance to them. This helped make the therapeutic space safe and nurturing. Neither Gina nor Beth had an active concern for the therapeutic space itself being unsafe. That was not a fear. However, they were afraid that it might not prove to be a productive time or nurturing space. They feared that their ultimate goal, of trying to find a space for discussion and support of their relationship and its relation to God, might not be accomplished in the therapeutic context.

Beth and Gina, at our initial interview, raised many questions about my approach to a variety of issues as a pastoral psychotherapist. We also discussed the topics of homosexual relations and relations in general. I explained to Gina and Beth both my own perspective and approach as pastoral psychotherapist and those of my denomination in answer to their questions. I tried to be as clear as possible about the nature and extent of the conflict involved. They appreciated receiving this information and we agreed that if necessary we might return to this topic in the therapeutic process. The relating of this information in answer to their questions and concerns helped greatly to address their stated fear concerning the therapeutic context. At the end of the initial session and during their movement through the first episode, Gina and Beth each expressed hope that this therapeutic context could be a context of support for their relationship and its relation to God. I encouraged them to work with this fear and use it as a therapeutic theme to which we could return to do assessment. This idea appealed to them, and as we progressed in the process we used this initial fear as a working assessment tool.

In the first episode of the process, Beth and Gina spoke openly about this fear and wanted to find active strategies for dealing with it. Attention to the creation of safe space helped to address this fear. The symbolic object that Gina brought was a wooden statue of a saint, one that she had carved when she was a teenager. The symbolic object that Beth brought was a paperweight from England. These objects had not only individual significance but also significance in the relationship. These objects and their reception helped make the therapeutic space one that could become trustworthy. The creation of safe therapeutic space when the therapist is dealing with a couple entails interaction between the therapist and both partners, and between the partners themselves.

Having the symbolic objects present provided a very helpful resource in our therapeutic time. These objects served a technical/practical function as well as a symbolic one. Gina had a tendency to ramble on and interrupt in therapy. Beth had a tendency to be reticent about speaking or to feel offended when Gina interrupted. Both women spoke about this and even laughed about it. At a session during the first month Beth had the idea of holding up their symbolic objects if either of them felt that the process somehow was being interrupted between themselves. This suggestion became an important part of the therapeutic process. When Beth felt that she was being interrupted, she would hold up her paperweight, and this would signal Gina to stop and let Beth finish. When Gina felt that Beth was reluctant to speak or was not joining the process enough, which was Gina's frequent complaint about Beth, she would hold up her symbolic object, the saint, and this would signal Beth that her input was needed. This use of the objects seemed to work, and it helped to minimize broken communication. The symbolic objects therefore not only helped by transforming the space into one that was safe and trustworthy but also helped as a communication signal in the therapeutic process itself. This multilevel strategy of using symbolic objects does not work in every case. However, it has proved useful when persons wish to engage it in the therapeutic context.

In the beginning Gina and Beth would take their objects home with them. Later on in the therapy they decided they wanted to leave them in the therapeutic space. The movement of these objects in and out of the therapeutic process became in itself a symbol of Gina's and Beth's movement in and out of their common and separate worlds. When strategies and exercises from the therapeutic context have an impact upon and can be tried and tested outside of that context, then therapeutic progress is being made in the life context in which people exist.

Episode 2. Entry Into Symbolic Reality

Both Gina and Beth were interested in discussing my approach to and theory of pastoral psychotherapy. As I explored these with them and encouraged their questioning, each expressed excitement about the process and the models out of which we would be working. Beth had brought in her own questions and ideas for the therapeutic process. She was concerned about the different roles of community and culture for her and Gina. Spending time on the models and identifying questions and concerns led to a way into the worlds of symbolic reality for Gina and Beth. Both Gina and Beth were very enthusiastic about understanding and becoming active partners in the process. Each was concerned that it *not* have, as Beth described, "a free-flowing and totally open orientation." Both women knew that they needed a process that could involve them at all levels and demand from them total engagement. They wanted therapy to be a critically caring challenge. The way of entry into Gina's system was quite different from Beth's. The understanding of this difference offered Beth and Gina a valuable insight into their different strategies and methods.

Gina was a person who entered her worlds visually; Beth was a person who entered her worlds through concepts and structures. As we discussed the means by which they formed meaning, the ways in which they approached problem solving, and the identification of issues, Gina and Beth had an opportunity to hear each other talk about their different ways of approach. The opportunity to speak and be heard concerning their ways of making meaning helped them better understand the differences in their approaches. This understanding stayed with them outside of the therapeutic time as they worked on different assignments and projects. Moving through this second episode lasted two months. This movement took us from the second month through the end of the third month. Entry into the symbolic realities of Beth and Gina happened in a complex and cyclical way. They became frustrated at times but did not run from that frustration. Through their commitment to try and figure out the ways in which they came to make meaning and the dimensions of that meaning-making, they better appreciated their differences. As they came to understand their different approaches, Beth and Gina identified for themselves exercises and assignments. This was a pattern they had used before in their relationship. We incorporated this exercise into the data-gathering task of symbolic reality for both women.

Gina identified a helpful pattern in her past and in her present, using imaging for an idea or for a disturbing thought that may have come into her mind. Through color, texture, and the tools of her trade as an artist, Gina found a way of making the idea or issue into an image, and working with it in a way that could move it from being tension-producing in a negative, elusive way to being tension-producing in a positive way. Gina's way of making meaning and moving through that meaning seemed natural for her. Once she identified this positive strategy, she began using it to sort through her current issues and tensions. Likewise, Beth had a strategy that had developed for her over time for sorting and assessing issues. Beth's strategy was somewhat parallel to Gina's in that it involved verbal images and word patterns. Certain words were able to translate tensions for her or place her in a different frame of mind.

Both Gina and Beth had employed these strategies before, but neither had given sustained thought to the profoundly useful nature of their strategies. As they began to do this in therapy, they were able to use these different strategies of meaning-making and, as Beth described it, "sanity-keeping," to reach greater depths of calm and clarity. The therapeutic process permitted and provided a place to talk about and understand the importance of these strategies. The use and encouragement of these strategies helped provide entry into symbolic reality. As each woman used her strategy, she was able to gather data about the different areas of symbolic reality in her life. The data emerged over several months. Preparation for entry into symbolic reality led to safe entry. This happened not only through the conscious process that each woman had undertaken, using the strategy of art or words, but also through the surfacing of memory-fragments in their recording of dreams. Both women had done journaling in the past of dreams and thoughts. Each began that process again as we reached this point of therapy. They also began carrying notebooks with them so that they could do their word-sketching or object-sketching during the day. Both expressed appreciation for the freedom and encouragement in the therapeutic context to identify helpful patterns from their past that they could now update and translate into dealing with the present. They engaged these patterns separately as well as together, as appropriate. During the second month we met once a week together, and, at their request, I also met individually with Gina and Beth. Each felt they wanted to do more intensive work on their own ways of entry into symbolic reality as they worked together.

Entering into the symbolic reality of the present was a fairly straightforward process for Gina. She named the personal resources of that reality including her relationship with Beth, her relationship with friends, and her relationship with work associates. The process of naming and finding ways of entry into the present symbolic reality for Beth was more complicated. Though she had a similar personal resource list that included Gina and friends, her work environment was not a resource. Whereas for Gina that current reality offered support and a group of associates, for Beth that current reality demanded secrecy and created a very real fear of being "discovered and tainted." Through this naming process, we were able to get a sense of the impact on Beth of her work environment with respect to her seeking to keep her personal life secret.

Having a safe space to talk about this and to express her sadness, anger, and grief led her to naming other environments in which she did not feel safe and from which she could not find support. For Beth, the Christian church and her experiences with it were another source of tension in her present symbolic reality. Her church experiences were more difficult to talk about than her work ones. Beth's faith was so vital to her life that being unable to find a community of faith in her present context had been very draining.

Entry into Beth's present symbolic reality, especially as she was able to talk about her church experiences, allowed entry into the symbolic reality of her past, her family of origin, her culture, and her community. Beth's pattern for looking at difficult issues was first to name and analyze them. Only after doing this could she begin to feel the emotions accompanying the issues. As Gina and I, in the therapeutic context, watched Beth move from a position of emotional distance to emotional contact, Beth became aware of how far apart she kept the different parts of herself. She worried about this, but Gina and I encouraged her not to be afraid of this and not to try to change things at this point. With this encouragement, Beth seemed to relax somewhat and prepared herself for the symbolic entry into her past. In the third month of the therapeutic process, Beth was able to discuss and analyze, but not enter emotionally, her past symbolic reality. Gina's support for Beth was very important. Gina was now able to understand better the consequences of the fear and terror that Beth had been living with for quite a while. A very powerful therapeutic moment happened toward the end of the third month. Beth expressed the desire to "enter into the reality of my past pain in this safe space." Beth was annoyed at herself that she could not already do this and did not understand why it was that she could name, discuss, and analyze quite clearly, but she could not enter into it.

At the same time as Beth was struggling with reaching her emotions, Gina became aware of an area of her life which had experienced a split between awareness and emotion. This area focused on the loss of her family of origin as a nurturing resource, a resource that had been important to her in her past. As both women, in terms of their own process, became aware of the critical distinction between awareness of something and ability to emotionally engage it, they together requested that we say a prayer at the end of the session that marked our third month of work together. This request was important because it allowed a vital resource of their symbolic reality to enter into and undergird the therapeutic process. Faith and spiritual life had been central resources for them. Though their church experiences and the underlying theological assumptions informing their experiences were part of the therapeutic problem for them, their faith and spiritual life needed to remain alive in and out of the therapeutic process to help them survive.

Prior to this they had spoken about the spiritual dimension of their lives, but it had not entered into the therapeutic process. As they reached this point of feeling almost at an impasse within themselves between present and past, analysis and emotion, their religious instinct made itself known. They had reached a point of weariness that could only be addressed by the infusion of spiritual hope. The prayer that ended this session was spontaneous except for its opening words, which they said together, "Our God, who art in heaven." The prayer itself was very powerful. It was a prayer that captured both their desperation and hopefulness. Both Beth and Gina were feeling desperate, yet with hope that their spiritual life and faith could help them at this point to find a way of entering into the pain and the very real frustration they were undergoing, being aware of pain and yet not being able to encounter it emotionally.

Episode 3. Identifying Central Strategies and Rituals of Symbolic Reality

The experience of the prayer in the therapeutic context was important for the therapeutic process. It was in itself an instance of a common and positive ritual that transformed the therapeutic context. In the following session there was a changed dimension. Beth noted this most clearly, "I feel a different energy here; I feel God is present." The sensing of God's presence allowed both women to trust that somehow they would find a way to, in Gina's words, "bring our minds and emotions, faith and church together, so we can live as human beings again."

The identification of central strategies and rituals in their symbolic reality had already begun for Gina and Beth. Obviously, one important ritual had already been enacted in the therapeutic context, and that was the use of prayer. Both women identified prayer as being a very central activity of their faith in their early childhood, in their adulthood prior to meeting each other, and since meeting each other. Gina and Beth were able to identify rituals, primarily of a religious nature, that had been significant to them as they moved through early childhood and adulthood.

For Gina, the experience of the Roman Catholic sacraments of confession, communion, and confirmation were powerful markers of the stages of her life. She found in those three rituals not just the memory of a powerful experience in the past but a source of spiritual energy that she could call upon in the present. This energy helped to calm her or to give her strength. Gina identified several situations in her life when she had called upon these ritual memories, for instance, when she was working on a difficult piece of art or when she was having difficulties with her parents. In these situations she recalled drawing upon the memory of the rituals and gaining strength from them. Gina remembered using the rituals' strength three years ago when she was going through the difficult separation from her family over her relationship with Beth. Gina remarked that she had attempted to call upon these rituals at this point in her life but that they were not working as they had in the past.

Gina was able to see that one reason why they were not working now in the same way was that she had never before experienced her symbolic reality coming face-to-face with a situation of rejection and terror. She had never before come up against a situation that threatened to put her faith itself at risk. Gina, in the safe context of pastoral therapy, was able to name her great-est fear: "that my God cannot accept me as I am, as a woman who loves an-other woman." Prior to this Gina had understood the rejection of the church and its theological assumptions but had not experienced the threat and terror. Now, in this pastoral context made safe by active participation, Gina could name the threat and terror and encounter them. This was her moment to come to terms with her fear. Gina knew that and expressed it in her own words: "God needed to help me fight this fear of God abandoning me." Through prayer, ritual memory, and ritual energy, Gina found ways to experi-ence God's presence with her, helping her through her fear.

As she prayed for God's help, Gina was now able to remember one of her own childhood rituals that she had forgotten. When she was growing up, before dinner on Sundays each member of the family had a special time of quiet in his or her own room. For Gina this time was always filled with dance. She found dance to be a happy and releasing activity even as a child. What she could not say in words, she could dance through movement. Sometimes she could dance for her family as her prayer part. Gina interpreted her recall of this memory as a sign from God for her to not lose strength. Though Gina did not want to bring her dance into therapy, she used dance at home to help her focus and gain strength.

The ritual identification process for Beth was similar to Gina's. Beth was able to recall not only particular rituals of religious significance, including the sacrament of communion, but also daily rituals, including prayer, that brought her into balance and stability in different situations of tension or uncertainty. When Beth began talking about the strategies and rituals of her past, she found that they often involved family activity. Her family served as the back-ground of the rituals and strategies. As Beth continued to probe the strategies and rituals of her past symbolic reality, her family emerged from background to foreground in a disturbing way. Beth experienced a feeling of distance and criticism as a child, both physical and emotional, from both of her parents. Beth struggled to name the loss that she was suffering through the estrange-ment from and abandonment by her family as a result of her relationship with Gina. This present loss brought to memory family religious rituals in which she felt excluded or insufficient. Both parents criticized Beth for being quiet and withdrawn. Beth remembered one time when she prayed a special prayer that she had written, and her father told her that "it was not suitable for God." Beth desperately yearned to find closeness with her father and her mother, but she found it virtually impossible. Beth painfully recalled activities and strategies that her mother used to silence her emotionally.

This pattern of distancing had continued through the years. The other children in the family were treated as she was. Beth's religious ritual experi-ences outside of her family helped offset the negative distancing of the family rituals. Within the church, which was at different points Presbyterian or Congregational, Beth found her ritual experience helpful and healing. The rituals she experienced in religious education and in Sunday church services—prayer, scripture study, and quiet reflection time—gave Beth a feeling of freedom and of belonging to God. What remained in her memory of these Sunday mornings in church school and in church services was the feeling of being loved by God and by those around her in contrast to what she had experienced in her cold and sterile home environment.

As Gina and Beth moved through this third episode, months four through six, engaging in memory recall of specific rituals and strategies, we took time to build a perspective in the present context to which both could return when they felt overwhelmed by past memories. Gina and Beth worked together to identify the functioning strategies and rituals that were happening in their life. They were very conscious of a desire to identify the strategies and rituals that they had constructed in their life together. These included their own Friday evening family ritual involving a prayer together, preparation of a common meal, and reflection time to bring their thoughts and concerns to God. Their work schedules were such that they rarely had a chance to be together Monday through Thursday. They planned an intentional Friday ritual, and this sustained them through the week. Their other ritual took place on a daily basis. Before they went to sleep, they would pray together.

These rituals proved to be very sustaining, and from them emerged various strategies that they used in their different life contexts. These rituals and strategies helped them build a strong present perspective from which to examine rituals of their past. However, as we began discussing and assessing the religious rituals that were currently in their life together, the deep distance they were experiencing from the larger religious structures became apparent. It was at this point that Gina and Beth chose to talk about their different church experiences in depth. They each had refrained from talking about these in therapy. They now felt able to do so because their current rituals were helping them keep balance and build strength with one another and God.

Gina and Beth, over the past three years, had tried numerous times and in different contexts to find a Christian church community that could support them as individuals and in their commitment together. They had struggled with the idea of not telling the truth about their relationship but decided that would not be wise. They often found a welcome for them as individuals but not as a couple. Whether or not their relationship was labeled "sin," the effect was the same. Both women mourned the absence of a spiritual community, a congregation of faith. Both felt committed to finding a community within the Christian church. Both had been deeply scarred by these experiences of rejection. The scarring did not lead either woman to abandon her faith, but led each to strengthen her relationship with God. This did not mean that there were no nights and days filled with doubts and fears. This did mean that the doubts and fears never destroyed their hope. As Beth and Gina talked about these experiences, at the end of the sixth month, they began to move into episode four and the assessing process.

Episode 4. Assessing the Impact of Strategies and Rituals on the Caring Process

Through episode four Gina and Beth continued to piece together memories of the past. They now became more involved with the process of assessing the impact of the strategies and rituals of the past and present on the way they felt about themselves, their relationship, and possibilities for the future. This kind of assessing process involved both intellect and emotions.

As Beth initially recalled memories in episode three, there seemed to be a great deal of positive energy surrounding her church experiences. However, as she began to organize this data and assess the impact of her childhood as a whole, she became overwhelmed at points at her feeling of being violated by her family, with the positive rituals of her church experience fading into the background. She summed up her childhood as having been "distorting, denying, and suffocating for my spirit." In the seventh month Beth described her childhood experience as being "that which tried to kill me."

Beth's moving through this fourth episode was difficult. It was not until well into the eighth month that she was able to set the assessment of negative childhood impact into some sort of perspective. As Beth allowed herself to assess the past through reexamining it in the therapeutic process, she could begin to develop her perspective. The reexperiencing of childhood memories took place in therapy. As Beth recalled certain experiences, I worked with her to reexperience them in the sessions. This reexperiencing was followed by an assessing process. For Beth this involved raising questions, naming, and devising her own set of labels to mark each experience on a large poster board. This was an energy-draining experience for Beth. I encouraged her to use her word drawings and to go for long walks in order to keep up her strength.

Though she took comfort in knowing she was in the *present* moving into an assessment of her *past*, Beth needed to find ways to stay in the present and not to be overcome by the impact of her past. At several points she felt exhausted and overwhelmed through month seven. Yet she still had some sense of being in the present. As we moved into the eighth month, Beth was able to feel that her assessing process of the negative impact of her past could be set to rest for a time. In large part she could do this because she had used all the means available in her assessing—she noted that "my mind, soul, and heart have been working." Both Gina and I encouraged Beth in this total engagement, and in a sense the encouragement gave Beth permission to approach her past with intensity. This intensity in the reexperiencing process offset the distancing, suffocating, and withdrawal patterns she remembered being negative strategies from her past. The process of going back into the past and assessing its impact was done within a present context of nurture and support.

For Beth the process of going back, reexperiencing, and assessing was therapeutic on several levels. The pastoral functions—healing, guiding, sustaining, and reconciling—helped Beth through this difficult period. At the end of month seven Beth asked me for spiritual care literature to read. I told her about the pastoral care functions and gave her a brief bibliography. She was fascinated by the historical functions. She found these functions useful for understanding what was happening for her in the therapeutic process. It was the first time that she felt able to guide herself, to go back and assess with God's love. The function of guiding, with Gina and me as companions working near but outside her symbolic reality circle, assisted Beth to be her own guide. Through the function of guiding, Beth was able to feel and to experience what it means to be able to create a perspective in the present for journeying into one's own past.

The function of healing for Beth was not as straightforward as guiding. Beth needed encouragement to trust that she could go into memory and do assessment without the memory destroying her in the present. Slowly, Beth was able to trust that she could do this at her own pace. Beth used prayer, scripture reading, and a variety of different techniques that were a part of her past but that she needed to reclaim in her present. The sense of healing and the healing process, as they became manifest, participated in the sustaining function. Beth's movement through the therapeutic process whereby Beth could remain in the present and assess her past helped her to feel balanced. Though it was a very difficult period for her, through our support and her hard work on building a perspective, Beth trusted that the impact of this assessment would not destroy her present. In prior attempts to look at her past she had not felt the safety or preparation to do this. She now felt able to sustain herself through faith and able to know how to ask for help to be sustained.

The reconciling function emerged as Beth moved from months seven to eight. The move marked Beth's ability to go from reconciling the negative impact of her past and the consequences of these past rituals to allowing room for looking at the positive rituals of her past as well, including her memories of church school and worship services. She could begin to reconcile the nurturing that had taken place along with the denial. By the end of month eight the process for Beth had come full circle to the present in terms of her ability to do the sorting, naming, and assessing necessary to be grounded in the present.

Gina's months seven and eight formed a slightly different pattern. Because Gina remembered the rituals and strategies of her past symbolic reality as very empowering and strengthening, her seventh month was filled with the work of trying to understand the various levels at which the positive impact of these past rituals affected her development, her way of looking at the world, and her sense of strength. Gina also identified the importance of her present rituals with Beth, present rituals with friends, and strategies from her work place that supported and nurtured her. Gina's seventh month also focused on witnessing and helping Beth through the struggles of difficult and painful assessment. This was important for Gina to do in order for her to understand both the agony that Beth had experienced as a child and the consequences that Beth now experienced from her past. The eighth month for Gina was one of active companioning of Beth.

The pastoral functions also helped Gina to be clearer about the forces from her past that had been resources for healing energy: prayer, art, dancing, family time, and early church experience. In terms of the guiding function, Gina's going back to past memory, being able to set a perspective from her past and in her present, and to do impact assessment were not new processes for Gina although she had not done these in this way before. She was used to being able to go through and set perspectives. She felt there was not much in her past through which she had to do sorting in terms of negative reconciling. She was skilled at reconciling the positive dimensions of her past and understanding their impact as sustaining her development.

In month eight, Gina experienced another dimension of the assessment process as the active companion to Beth as Beth was going through her assessment process. As Beth began the assessment process, Gina chose to companion Beth. In order to do this, Gina and I also worked individually for two sessions. After that, we paused with our individual work. This was done very consciously because we all felt it would be important to work through the assessment of past rituals and strategies together. What Gina discovered as we entered the eighth month was that she needed to concentrate energy in order to create a perspective that incorporated both distance from and closeness to Beth.

Gina found it difficult to stay at a critical distance from Beth in order for Beth to do her own assessment. Beth wanted Gina present but knew she needed to do this work herself. Beth had to keep reminding Gina to, in Beth's words, "not come too close just now." Gina's tendency was, as she expressed it, "to jump in and take the pain away from Beth." Beth was able to move from past to present and say to Gina, "That will not help me." This was a powerful process to watch. In this process empowering went both ways. Beth needed to be there to help Gina know the limits of helpfulness, and Gina needed to be there to offer strength and nurture to Beth. Gina found herself relearning the pastoral functions through Critical Caring with another human being: healing—helping someone, companioning someone, and allowing the other to experience the pain as part of healing; guiding—being present and supporting but trying not to spare another the difficult process of setting up a perspective; reconciling—resisting the desire to fuse the past and present, blurring the positive and negative memories of past ritual; and sustaining—naming, recognizing, and appreciating the differences between people to make maximum use of differences as resources and not as dividers in a relationship.

Episode 5: Bringing Strategies and Rituals Into the Therapeutic Context and Discovering Ways for Containing

Discovering ways for containing ritual memory and energy took place for Gina and Beth from the beginning of the ninth month through the thirteenth month of therapy. Over this time period I worked with Gina and Beth separately and together. The patterns and rhythms needed for this point in our work together were discussed at length in our first session that marked the ninth month together. Both Beth and Gina felt that their prior work on assessing and their working through the companioning part that accompanied that process had brought them to a point where they needed to work on issues about rituals and strategies separately.

Beth and Gina needed space from each other to work toward containment. Beth wanted to work on containing rituals and strategies from her past and present. She wanted to attempt to do some reconstruction of the rituals from her past, both the negative and positive ones, in order to better understand how they triggered the kind of emotional impact that she had identified earlier. Gina felt she needed to continue working on the dimension of rituals and strategies from her past and present whereby she could work on the conscious ability to create and keep responsible distance. Gina understood that in her past relationships this blurring of the critical distance line was something that she had experienced but had not comprehended as a point of concern. Gina was finding now, especially in her relationship with Beth, that she needed to work on a new approach to critical distance.

In our sessions together during this stage the following pattern was established. Beth and Gina would spend time informing one another about what they thought important from their individual sessions and what in their containment and ritual work of reconstruction would be of importance to their relationship. Much of the therapeutic time in this fifth episode concentrated on ways in which Beth and Gina could develop both the critical and the caring dimensions of their relationship.

Through this process each discovered that what had been happening in the present was to some degree a magnification of the tendencies each brought from their past. Gina's tendency was to care uncritically; this kind of uncritical caring of Beth led Gina, as she described it, "to try and take over for her." On the other hand at points of stress and tension, Beth's tendency was to distance herself from Gina to the point where caring was impeded. Hearing their tendencies voiced allowed Gina and Beth to approach these without the defensiveness they had experienced in the past. In a moment of humorous exchange at the end of the ninth month, Beth described her tendency as "critical uncaring." Gina described her tendency as "uncritical caring." Through their laughter they found release, and each found the term "Critical Caring" to be a challenge to undertake. Each desired to find her place on a Critical Caring continuum.

Moving into episode five did not entail for Beth and Gina an abrupt change from what we had been doing but simply a moving on to the next step. From the beginning of our time together, Beth and Gina had occasionally brought with them different symbolic objects. In the beginning of the therapeutic process these objects were used to create a safe therapeutic space. At this point in the process when both Beth and Gina had identified rituals and patterns with which they wanted to work, I especially encouraged them to find objects or symbols that could help them bring these ritual patterns and memories more poignantly and physically into the therapeutic context. For both women this was a relatively easy process. Each already had in her own life and their life together a number of symbolic objects that helped them to work on framing and containing issues. As was true in each episode of the process, the containing stage for Beth and for Gina had to be engaged in differently. The rhythm of individual and joint sessions allowed Beth and Gina to work together on their separate assignments or joint assignments during their times between sessions.

For Beth who was battling against her memories and rituals of distancing and denial, the process of containing took the form of deciphering what kind of critical question she needed to ask of herself. Beth developed her own question around the containing process: "How can I know who or what to let into my world?" After voicing this question, Beth seemed somewhat surprised by it. Her surprise was at her own ability to develop this question. "A part of me thought I was doomed to always be trapped in isolation inside. I felt like there were few life lines of connection left. It is a surprise to come up with my own question of how to let things in." Her question proved pivotal during the next months. When Beth found herself, in her own words, "at a stuck place," she would go back to her own critical question for containment, of deciphering how to "let in."

For Gina the "letting in" point of the containment process had not presented itself as difficult. Instead, learning to appreciate the need for and ability to construct appropriate boundaries became Gina's focus. Her critical question became "How can I limit without seeing it as pulling away?" When Gina heard herself ask the question, she was surprised how clearly she could name what was working in her. An important dimension of being able to work with Gina and Beth jointly while they were exploring their own critical questions individually was that in hearing the other's critical question each became a creative listener in the other's process. Both in and out of the therapeutic context there was a living resource for Beth and Gina in each other, having found another who had heard the question and could offer strength to find its answer.

During this episode Beth's individual containing work incorporated a number of physical objects and symbols including some from her past, from her childhood. Beth found it helpful to give particular memories an object association in the therapeutic context. She had recalled ten pivotal memories dealing with either the more negative impact of distancing or with the positive impact of nurturing through her church experience. For each of these memories she named a particular object as its keeper. The objects included dolls, books, rocks, and pieces of art. Beth requested we pray for these objects to be blessed, to be set aside for helping her accomplish her task. Once Beth felt at home with her objects, she developed her own working strategy whereby she would think of a memory, pick up the object, and talk to it. She imbued the object not only with the memory from the past but also with her hope for learning how to contain it.

As Beth began to realize how the objects were functioning, she started to develop an imbuing process within herself, within her mind, her body, and her soul. And through these months Beth was able to move toward internalizing the containing process. She still wanted and needed to have her objects, "my imbued objects" as she called them, yet they moved more and more to the periphery as she learned how to contain internally. In my work with Beth, I encouraged her to use resources from the safe parts of her present to help with the containing process. Beth at first liked this idea but could not think of anything to use. We let this idea rest. While it rested, Beth worked with other resources. Then, around month eleven, Beth began to bring in some of the tools with which she worked in her business. These work tools eventually became tools for the containment process. This proved significant for Beth because it allowed her work context to enter into the therapeutic context. This helped also to contain the uncomfortable and unsafe dimension of her work context, the keeping of her personal life and her relationship with Gina secret. Bringing in objects from work gave Beth a greater sense of confidence. This did not mean that she did or should let go of the suspicions she had about her work context. More will be said on this in terms of a joint ritual and strategy containment process.

The individual containing process of strategies and rituals for Gina also involved bringing in a variety of different objects that symbolized her world and helped her to set limits without interpreting them as blocks to intimacy in the caring process. Gina also used her drawings and different dances as part of this process because these were her ways of symbolizing things to herself. Gina was surprised at how difficult this work of setting limits was for her. It was at this point in the therapeutic process that Gina began to recall memories of some of the more uncomfortable moments from her late childhood and adolescence where she felt critical distance had not been maintained. She recalled various instances when she felt she had needed more privacy in her household and when she felt uncomfortable with her father's awareness of her as a growing young woman. Although she did not recall any instances of her father abusing her or of the lack of privacy as being unbearable, she realized that she had a somewhat different sensibility about distance than her family but that she did not have a chance to express this.

These memories surfaced as Gina began to identify an area that she knew was problematic in her relationship with Beth but also in other relationships. It was also at this point, during month eleven, that Gina surfaced some current concerns she was having at work. These involved conflicts over joint projects and issues that concerned several staff members. Each of these situations involved Gina's need to create greater critical distance. Gina's greatest fear was, that in trying to set limits, she would offend others. Gina and I worked actively on this fear, having her test some of her new strategies for setting limits in her work environment. She also tried to imagine different ways she could develop this kind of critically important limit setting in terms of her relationship with Beth.

In the twelfth month, at a joint session in which Gina and Beth were discussing their challenges to work on containment, there arose concern about the need to contain a particular grief each woman separately and both together were experiencing. The focal point of this grief was the absence of a place of Christian worship where they could express their faith. The discussion was difficult, but each expressed her deep need to grieve. Neither knew quite how to do this. Both had thought that through conversation the grief would be lightened. This did not happen. Beth and Gina asked for my help with the task of grieving. Finally, we all decided that a grieving service was needed. Beth and Gina planned a very intricate grieving ritual to take place within the pastoral therapeutic context at the end of the twelfth month. They requested having others present. Each invited one close friend, and together they invited two mutual friends.

The ritual was planned to take place within the normal time frame of our session. Gina and Beth each planned to bring a representative sampling of their symbolic objects. They each prepared to use sections of the funeral service from their different denominational liturgies. We discussed the role that I would play in this. I was not sure what role they expected me to play, nor was I sure of the role that would be most appropriate. We jointly decided that I would be present as a member of the Christian clergy as well as their pastoral therapeutic partner. They requested my presence in both capacities. I concurred. We worked together on the liturgical and prayer dimensions of the ritual.

Once the ritual format was set, Gina and Beth worked on the details of the service. They involved their friends as witnesses and participants in the grieving process. Each person was asked to bring an object that would be put into a special box representing, in Beth's words, "the pain, estrangement, loss, and grief over a home of faith." The ritual itself took about twenty minutes, followed by some light refreshments. It took place at the end of our session. Beth and Gina left with their friends at the conclusion of the ritual. The wooden box was kept on a shelf in my office for the remainder of our time together.

The impact of this grieving ritual on the therapeutic process was felt at two levels. First, it assisted Gina and Beth in understanding the consequences of being without a faith community. Beth and Gina frequently made reference to the impact of the ritual as a new memory for them that they could recall to contain and sometimes counter a whole variety of memories from the past and in the present.

Second, the grieving ritual had a profound impact on my own theological and pastoral understanding. Involvement in the ritual as ritual co-participant, and not only as observer, created an experience of ritual impact I had not fully anticipated. It seems appropriate to discuss briefly the impact here, as this material itself would later serve a function in the therapeutic process.

As a *pastoral* therapist I had to come to grips with the pain and deep spiritual as well as psychological scarring caused by theological rejection; the theological challenge of seeing the nature of a woman-to-woman or man-to-man relationship as being a positive expression of relationship between adults; and the quality of care between persons as being the responsible, theological assessment measure of relationship. As a theologian located in the context of a denomination that at best does not understand such a relationship to be acceptable and at worst labels such as sin, I found myself in a difficult position. I most certainly could not, theologically or professionally, attach a label of sin to this relationship. I found myself being confronted with the consequence of theological labeling in a way that I had not before. Confronting the agony and grief in the lives of Gina and Beth made the naming of this consequence vital. The consequence was a form of theological terror, affecting every level of their lives. As a pastoral psychotherapist I found myself faced with a challenge to confront theology's legacy of terror. Undertaking this challenge was possible through the support of colleagues in two networks: clinical and theological.

At the time I was working actively on this, neither the timing nor my own containment of the process was appropriate for bringing this experience into the therapeutic context. It had no direct bearing on Gina's and Beth's progress at this point in the therapeutic process. However, my assessment changed toward the end of our thirteenth month, when I had resolved a plan of action for addressing the theological challenge and had sufficiently contained the multilevel issues that had surfaced.

At this later point in the therapeutic process, in my critical judgment and that of my colleagues, it seemed most appropriate to the rhythm of the process to let Gina and Beth know the challenge I had faced and resolved. I shared with them briefly my own process—for the following reasons. First, I wanted to be open about the need for therapists in general and pastoral therapists in particular to see themselves as human, as living human beings and not as distant experts. Second, it seemed a helpful way to make the point that one never really reaches a point where the process of being challenged by experience, by information, by one's own memories, by the process of affiliations, whatever, leaves one free from tensions. Third, in the face of tensions, a challenge is created and it is possible to work through an issue to find resolution. Fourth, and most importantly, this provided an experience that we could examine together to better understand the Critical Caring process and its dimensions.

They found my willingness to talk about this experience very important and very liberating for them. I found it important and liberating for myself. After this exchange and the discussion it brought, one of the greatest points of Critical Caring occurred in the therapeutic process. They trusted their own strength and faith to try again to find a community of faith that could be caring of and with them. Gina and Beth greatly appreciated our discussion of my struggle, and it helped them to articulate an idea for moving from the present into the future.

Gina's and Beth's work on and movement through past ritual remembrance and ritual assessment to the construction of the grief ritual led them to a point of readiness to mobilize resources toward the future. In light of this, and the positive impact of the grief ritual, they requested another ritual, one of blessing for their relationship. This request came in the fourteenth month of therapy as Gina and Beth moved toward developing new memories and rituals.

Episode 6. Developing Means for Creating New Memory, New Ritual

Gina's and Beth's request for a blessing ritual came as they made the decision to investigate and locate theologically, individually, and cooperatively a faith community with which to affiliate. I encouraged them to think about broadening their search of faith communities. Since they came from different traditions, they needed to look at a variety of theological and denominational issues. This search stretched over a three-month period. As we worked on the investigating dimension in therapy, Beth and Gina visited thirty different faith communities.

During month sixteen of the therapeutic process they finally found a small Episcopal congregation that seemed welcoming of them. The pastor and church members were quite open to having Gina and Beth as active church members individually and jointly. This welcoming was very significant in itself, and it came at a point when Beth's and Gina's hopes for finding a place of worship were almost exhausted. Gina and Beth were not feeling certain that they could find a place of worship and community. Through these months of investigation, Gina and Beth found strategies for better understanding their theological concerns and issues. It had been painful but important for them to work together on creating and containing their hope for finding a community of faith that could understand their theological concerns. To sustain Beth and Gina in this period, we devised strategies similar to those used earlier. Beth worked at not closing herself off entirely but trying to leave lines of hope open. Gina was intent at setting more limits and trying to contain her energy. These efforts allowed Beth to be open to finding a community now or later and Gina not to be totally devastated and disappointed if one could not be found. When they finally found a community of faith that welcomed them, we celebrated with a prayer ritual of thanksgiving.

The rhythms and strategies that Beth and Gina had developed were proving useful for them. As they explored their new Christian community of faith, we had to come to terms with another context of tension, and that was the very different nature of their work situations. We all felt it useful to use these strategies to explore their work contexts. Using these strategies helped us to identify and organize the difficult issues. Whereas Gina's work context had been generally one of support and openness, sometimes to the extreme, Beth's had been one that made her feel unsafe in terms of her personal life and her relationship with Gina. Interestingly, their work environments seemed to parallel their individual rhythms: Gina's need for limits and Beth's need for openness. However, the safety factor for Beth marked the critical difference.

It was easier in some ways for Beth to imagine Gina's setting because she had visited the building many times. Gina had spent far less time at Beth's place, so this was one of the assignments that they undertook. Gina would visit Beth's place more often and by herself. Though Beth might be there, they chose not to share the link between themselves in the public setting. Gina and Beth worked together to read different published stories of lesbian and gay people struggling to exist in negative environments. The forced silence and secrecy issues emerging from the literature helped identify the deepest pain for Beth. Gina began to understand Beth's situation at a deeper level. There seemed nothing more to do about this at the moment. However, the effort given to understanding their work contexts and their consequences gave new strength to both women.

At the end of the seventeenth month, Beth and Gina were attending the Episcopal church regularly. As part of their getting to know the congregation and the congregation's getting to know them, they had shared parts of their story. Beth and Gina had met with the priest several times, and he asked if he could help them in any way. They were feeling more and more welcomed in the community and asked about involving the priest and perhaps some members of their congregation in a ritual of commitment. They were very excited about this possibility and felt that they wanted to do this. They asked me if I could talk to the priest as well. I told them, "Yes, within the [therapeutic] limits that I feel I can."

In the middle of the eighteenth month, Gina and Beth in conjunction with the priest created a special service of commitment and blessing for their relationship. They had written vows and different elements of the service. My part in the service was to bear witness and to say a prayer of blessing. One therapy session was spent discussing the ritual. Their priest was invited for part of this session, and he expressed appreciation for this invitation. His presence was an important link for Beth and Gina. They had done much work in the therapeutic context to create links between the present and the future. Their priest's willingness and eagerness to be part of the therapeutic process allowed for a new memory to be formed and pastoral caring to be experienced. It gave the ritual of commitment and blessing, which took place at the church, a context of care and hope.

In the final month together, Gina, Beth, and I often referred to their commitment ritual. In this nineteenth month of the therapeutic process, Beth and Gina had a renewed sense of hope and purpose. In large part this was due to their being part of a faith community, a community of Critical Caring. The hope and purposefulness were accompanied by a new energy that helped them plan ways to support each other. Beth and Gina found new strategies to use, and Beth found a co-worker with whom she felt she might be able to talk about her relationship. Beth devised her own way of assessing whether or not this would be a worthwhile project. Gina encouraged Beth. Beth soon had one person in her work environment with whom she could share this very significant part of her life.

In our final session together, we chose to have a closing ritual. Gina and Beth brought their symbolic objects, and we gathered in a circle, saying prayers. Both Gina and Beth chose passages from scripture to read. We ended our time together on a note of hope, trusting in the containment of the strategies and rituals of the past and in the continued exploration of present rituals. In their closing prayers, each was able to move into the future with hope.

> *Beth's Prayer:* Lord, help me to be open and to trust that I will know what is safe. Thank you for getting us here to therapy and able to go on with our lives. I have learned how to trust myself and hope again.

> *Gina's Prayer:* God, thank you for your love and strength and for guiding us here to do this work. Keep us in your heart as we live our love for each other. Give us wisdom, patience, and an appreciation for limits.

CHAPTER 8

Closing Reflections and Additional Applications for the Clinical Model of Critical Caring

Reflections on Use of the Clinical Model of Critical Caring

As the journeys through these four case applications of the clinical model reveal, the model needs to remain as flexible as possible if it is to be effective. Development of a working partnership between pastoral therapist and person in therapy will provide the foundation for the model's direction and use. The more that a person can transform the model to her or his understanding and use, the greater the resource it will prove to be.

In my work with persons at different stages of the life cycle, the model, which represents my operating approach to the pastoral psychotherapeutic process, becomes a part of my explanation of what I do and how I do it. I usually try to do this in the introductory session when the person and I are trying to gather as much information as possible about each other and about the process in order to make a decision about working together. Many persons who have been in other therapeutic contexts are somewhat surprised by a therapist who is so willing to explain her orientation to the therapeutic process. However, in one way or another, if the therapeutic process is to continue, this kind of information needs to be shared. And this sharing models the dialogue necessary for Critical Caring.

In conjunction with talking about the clinical model, and sometimes the hermeneutical model as well, I introduce the idea of responsible scavenging. This image seems to be a very adaptable and useful metaphor and tool. Many

145

choose to create drawings of themselves as a responsible scavenger using different animal and abstract forms.

When therapy ends, the therapeutic work is naturally not finished. In therapy one will come to learn and/or create different ways of approach to the past and present, scavenging for resources, containing dangerous memory, and using rituals and symbols. By so doing, the therapeutic process and its techniques may continue to be engaged throughout the life of the person. In this sense experience in therapy and involvement in the psychotherapeutic process are in themselves actions of preventive care. The work of therapeutic healing and caring can continue long after the therapeutic time is over.

In the cases of Beth, Gina, Laura, Anna, and Heather I have been privileged to receive different communications from them years after the time in therapy has finished. The therapeutic resources, especially those dealing with symbols and rituals, have become a part of their lives. They use them as resources on a daily basis to do their own responsible scavenging and caring. I include a portion of one of Heather's communications as illustrative:

> We had our birthday party today, we are 9. Henry and I had a great cake which Mommy and Daddy made in the shape of the dancing butterfly. Henry and I think about butterflies a lot. He has a collection of them and just got a nice book about them. I got a book about them too, but I like to imagine them dancing around. For Halloween Mommy made me a butterfly costume but I use it to dance in all the time. Do you remember the dance we did that day? I wish we had made a video of it, but I can play it back in my mind anytime. Sometimes when I am sad I think about that day and also our little talks. It's like God gives me the memory to help me, and then I dance after. I hope one day you can come to our birthday and dance with us. I'll help you because I know it's not so easy for you to dance like me.

The Clinical Model as Development Resource for the Pastoral Psychotherapist

From a pastoral feminist perspective, as from every other therapeutic perspective, self-study and self-assessment are vital to the maintenance of a responsible clinical orientation. The pastoral feminist perspective demands this in its hermeneutical, theoretical, and clinical expressions. However, finding adequate resources whereby this study and assessment can be done is not always easy. It is not simply a matter of finding instruments or methods to use, although this in itself is difficult, but, just as important, one must have professional partners for this work.

Though each case and therapeutic situation has led me to look again at the clinical and hermeneutic models for my own orientation and perspective, the case of Beth and Gina proved to be one of the most challenging. It raised issues and questions at deep levels of my theological and professional identity.

The pastoral psychotherapist as a practitioner in the theological field needs to accept and undertake theological challenges when presented. If a difference of interpretation or a conflict arises between one's psychological and theological hermeneutic foundations, the pastoral psychotherapist needs to embrace the challenge offered by this difference or conflict. This kind of challenge is best undertaken in the context of community. In order to move ahead with the therapeutic process with Beth and Gina, I deliberately undertook the challenge presented through meeting with three different professional, psychological, and pastoral psychotherapeutic communities. In each community setting we used the model of Critical Caring to help us organize and address the different issues involved. This process needed the dialogue of community. The model's emphasis on dialogue and partnership applied to my situation and struggle as well as to the client's journey. Use of the model in community helped me to find resolution in order to continue in the therapeutic relationship and with the therapeutic work.

The Pastoral Feminist Process of Critical Caring and Challenges to Theology

If one begins from the understanding of pastoral psychology as part of the theological enterprise, then one should prepare a strategy for interaction with this enterprise. As stated in the first chapter, pastoral psychology and its subfields of caring have a unique position in the theological enterprise. It is in these contexts of care that the worldview and truth claims of theology intersect with the lives and experiences of persons struggling to understand and live their faith. This intersection brings together the worlds of the conceptual and the actual. Approach to the intersection needs to be carefully planned. One needs a road map, as it were, and an understanding of the different vehicles represented by these different worlds.

The meeting of worlds at this intersection is sometimes peaceful and ordered but often disturbing and confusing. Critical questions need to be raised and standards of evaluation need to be organized for both worlds. We initially and continually have before us the question: What is a sound theology? From a pastoral feminist perspective the answer is clear. A sound theology is one that assumes responsibility for its conceptual translation into the actual world of human living. A sound theology is one that understands and empowers Critical Caring and the nurture of the religious and relational instincts. A sound theology accepts challenge and embraces it and more: it takes an active role in addressing situations in the actual world in which uncaring has become the working methodology.

One means for the work of a sound theology is through pastoral psychology. And the pastoral psychotherapist, as working theologian, must find a way to raise concerns, issues, and questions with other theologians. This can be done in any number of ways. Structurally, the experiences and insights of the academic theologian, the pastoral theologian, the pastoral practitioner, and the person in the local church need to inform each other. A pastoral feminist model demands this as does the definition of a sound theology.

For those who are able and choose to undertake the challenge of working across the hermeneutical, theoretical, and clinical dimensions of pastoral psychology, the undertaking is often exhausting and always demanding. However, the challenge to work in this way can bring unparalleled opportunity and intellectual excitement as well. In my experience this undertaking has worked best when it is located in the context of an ongoing resource network of scholars, clinicians, and pastors all struggling and working together to do the responsible scavenging necessary to be accountable theologians.

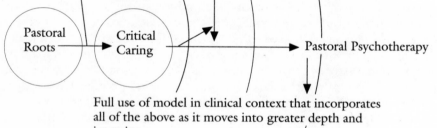

Pastoral Pyschology

Pastoral Care

Use of model by caregiver for assessing nature of symbols and rituals to be used in pastoral work. Working with person and with community at her/his/their developmental levels to help them understand symbols. Networking with persons to understand consequences of past religious events or theological symbols. Exploration of church space and safe places for spiritual exercises and quiet meditation.

Pastoral Counseling

All of the above for pastoral care and, in addition, beginning the exploration of symbolic reality and functioning symbols of faith and caring. Perhaps beginning work with creating perspective and the working of critical distance. Using symbols and rituals collaboratively with persons marking adjustments or transitions in life and faith. Exploration of space and dimensions of safe space for work of faith.

Pastoral Roots → Critical Caring → Pastoral Psychotherapy

Full use of model in clinical context that incorporates all of the above as it moves into greater depth and intensity.

Preventive Care   Intensive Care
Increasing in Intensity

Diagram 7. Model of Critical Caring Applied and Adapted in the Different Pastoral Contexts

Application of the Critical Caring Model in Other Pastoral Contexts

The nature of the clinical model of Critical Caring is a resource for analysis and assessment of self and others in and through the context of faith and community. As such, it is not an exclusive tool for the multilevel and intensive work of pastoral psychotherapy. It is, in fact, a preventive care resource that can be used at all levels of intensity for the umbrella fields of pastoral psychology. No matter where a person may be developmentally or what situation presents itself for action, the model may be of use. It allows for the pastoral partners to find a way of entry and a means for interpreting symbols and events in a person's life. And it allows a person to decipher the dimensions and stages of her or his spiritual and personal life. Let us briefly return to the diagram of pastoral psychology as a field introduced in the first chapter, here presented with suggestions for using the Critical Caring model in pastoral work at all levels (see diagram 7).

Closing Note

In a volume such as this, a final word of invitation seems appropriate. To those colleagues in pastoral psychology or related fields this invitation is to experiment with and make use of the models offered here. It is hoped that you may use them as a way to raise critical questions and continue the responsible scavenging process to which pastoral psychology challenges us.

Notes

Chapter 1

1. The work of William A. Clebsch and Charles R. Jaekle, *Pastoral Care in Historical Perspective*, provides a well-known discussion of the functions in relation to pastoral care; see especially 67–82 for discussion of pastoral functions in the context of different historical periods. See also John McNeill's *A History of the Cure of Souls* for an understanding of the cure of souls in historical and denominational perspective.

2. The transition from care of the soul understood as the cure of soul to the more contemporary concern for the whole person is a long and multi-leveled journey spanning centuries of time as well as shifting cultural and social worldviews. Time and focus do not allow for an exploration of this important journey here. The reader can begin an exploration of different dimensions of this journey in Clebsch and Jaekle, *Pastoral Care in Historical Perspective*, especially 11–31. See also Brooks Holifield's *A History of Pastoral Care in America* for an excellent overview of theological and social developments and transitions shaping the nature and evolution of pastoral care.

3. The understandings offered here of what pastoral psychology is and where it is located as a field as well as the idea of it having three subfields are not to be assumed as the framework of definition or identification for other pastoral psychology investigations. Yet where we begin in our process of definition and location is crucial for the consistency and evolution of where we hope to go.

Understanding the importance of articulating points of orientation for pastoral psychology is vital for the academic, theoretical, and practical workings of the field. For a very interesting article on the location and orientation of pastoral psychology and the pastoral field that begins and ends with a significantly different operating perspective see Donald S. Browning, "Introduction to Pastoral Counseling," 5–13.

4. Perhaps there is just as much controversy surrounding the thesis of "expected" developmental stages as there is in the thesis that they do not exist. Therefore I prefer to think of development as a progression, having some overall features for human beings, but always being a product of culture, belief system, and psychosocial orientation. This orientation allows for different progressions across cultures or even within a culture concerning gender development or other differences.

5. The important point here is that the person or persons are designated and recognized by the faith community and thus represent the community and are entrusted with the community's symbols of sacrament and ritual. In their definition of pastoral care, Clebsch and Jaekle, *Pastoral Care in Historical Perspective*, 4, include the phrase, "representative Christian persons." Though there has been controversy in contemporary applications of this historical part of the definition, the point to be underscored here is the emphasis on the representational and recognized aspects of the persons who are entrusted with the symbols of the faith community. Functionally, if we place emphasis on the community's understanding of a representative person, then this leaves the nature of the representation open to community clarification.

6. The nature of this training is being coordinated and supervised by organizations such as the American Association of Pastoral Counselors and its training programs and centers. However, this in itself does not address the concern for the interpretive framework being used and the nature and role of pastoral being assumed. Browning in his "Introduction to Pastoral Counseling," 7, makes the following observation: "There are also within this tradition [pastoral psychotherapy] widely shared assumptions about the nature of human nature and the fundamental character of the world. These moral and religious attitudes constitute the assumptive background of pastoral psychotherapy." At the theoretical and academic levels, this may be thought or assumed. However, this is not always the case at the clinical level for pastoral psychotherapists. In the words of one professional colleague:

> Through my training and now in my own work supervising pastoral therapists in training, it has been and remains a struggle to find a place for the pastoral concerns in pastoral psychotherapy. Concerns about human nature and deep theological issues are not translated into the work we do and often are not functional parts of the training curriculum. I hope that future training programs will not continue in this way. Pastoral needs to enter in, not just be added on to psychotherapy.

7. A helpful discussion of the role of culture and community is found in Arthur Kleinman's *Patients and Healers in the Context of Culture*, especially 24–25.

8. The *Oxford English Dictionary*, 2d ed., s.v. "scavenge" and "scavenger." See also *Webster's Third New International Dictionary*, s.v. "scavenge" and "scavenger."

9. The *Oxford English Dictionary*, 2d ed., s.v. "critic" and "critical," and "critically." See also *Webster's Third New International Dictionary*, s.v. "critic" and "critical."

10. *The Oxford English Dictionary*, 2d ed., s.v. "care." See also *Webster's Third New International Dictionary*, s.v. "care."

11. Recognition of this division is clear. Numerous sources discuss this from different vantage points. I recommend Carol Gilligan's *In a Different Voice* as a helpful reference text as she examines the gender-associated divisions from a psychosocial and developmental theory perspective.

12. This is most clearly developed in Jungian theory with the feminine and masculine, and by association female and male, being understood as a complementary pair. There are numerous references to this in Jung. See especially material from Jung's *Collected Works*, vol. 7, pars. 250–400. However, as has been shown by numerous scholars, especially those working from a feminist perspective, complementarity does not imply equality and in fact has as its consequence inequality and sexism. See, for example, Wehr's "Religious and Social Dimensions of Jung's Concept of the Archetype, 23–45.

13. Though there are many theories responsible for this orientation, Freud's theory is perhaps the most significant. For an excellent analysis of the nature and consequences of his theory set in cultural perspective, see Judith van Herik's *Freud on Femininity and Faith*, especially 9–52.

14. For an insightful discussion of the consequences of domination through the analysis of gender–asymmetry, see van Herik's *Freud on Femininity and Faith*, 29–39, and her article, "The Feminist Critique of Classical Psychoanalysis," 83–84.

15. Words of an adult man in pastoral psychotherapy, a survivor of childhood abuse and neglect.

16. See the references to *The Oxford English Dictionary*, 2d ed., and *Webster's Third New International Dictionary* in notes 9 and 10 above.

17. Feminist scholarship is not the creation of women only. However, this work draws primarily on the work of women as they have supplied the primary insights shaping both the deconstructive and reconstructive feminist tasks throughout the academic and clinical areas.

18. See Elisabeth Schüssler Fiorenza's distinction in "The Will to Choose or to Reject," 135.

Chapter 2

1. See Susan Sturdivant's discussion of the nature of therapy and values in her work *Therapy with Women*, 10–29.

2. The use of hermeneutics and the focus on using a framework of interpretation for theology and psychology in pastoral psychology have become an operating standard for most contemporary texts in the field. See for example Charles Gerkin's *The Living Human Document,* especially 143–160.

3. My use of these texts in no way constitutes a review or analysis of them. They serve as reference points from which my work begins. Translation, as it were, of the concepts into the field of pastoral psychology alters the concepts from their original presentation. As expressed previously, these texts have become resources for my work in pastoral psychology, and therefore I assume responsibility for the products created with reference to them.

4. Sturdivant, *Therapy with Women,* 7.

5. Please see page 27 for dimensions of worldview.

6. Sturdivant, *Therapy with Women,* 9.

7. This is a crucially important alteration of the model and not a simple addition of theology to philosophy. Once theology is set in the context of the model, its presence becomes a foundation for the levels of theory and technique built upon it.

8. Ninian Smart, *Worldviews,* 2.

9. Elisabeth Schüssler Fiorenza, *In Memory of Her,* 3.

10. Both academic and clinical colleagues voiced some concern over the use of the word "instinct." It is hardly a popular word for those in pastoral psychology or related fields of inquiry. However, despite these appreciated concerns, I found myself returning again and again to the term. I could not find a better term to relate the meaning I wanted to convey.

11. *Dorland's Illustrated Medical Dictionary,* 27th ed., s.v. "instinct."

12. *The Oxford English Dictionary,* 2d ed., s.v., "instinct."

13. *Dorland's Illustrated Medical Dictionary,* 27th ed., s.v. "instinct."

14. For an excellent discussion of the tensions and challenges between a scientific and philosophical perspective of approaching definitions of health and illness, and the responsibility of hermeneutical inquiry see Henrik Wulff, Stig Andur Pedersen, and Raben Rosenberg, *Philosophy of Medicine,* especially 121–171.

15. Eugene Gendlin, "A Philosophical Critique of the Concept of Narcissism," 262.

16. Judith van Herik, *Freud on Femininity and Faith,* 191–192.

17. Ann Ulanov and Barry Ulanov, *Religion and the Unconscious,* 35.

18. Demaris Wehr, "Religious and Social Dimensions of Jung's Concept of the Archetype," 32.

19. Miriam Greenspan, *A New Approach to Women and Therapy,* 16.

20. Ibid., 21.

21. Ibid., 26.

22. See especially Bell Hooks, *Feminist Theory from Margin to Center,* for a clear and challenging discussion of power and race in feminist perspective.

23. See especially Beverly Harrison's "The Power of Anger in the Work of Love" for a discussion of the need for responsible anger to address issues of social and personal injustice.

24. "Central" does not rule out the existence of other instincts but does indicate the instincts that are most crucial for understanding human nature.

25. Peter Homans, "Toward a Psychology of Religion," 68. Homans discusses the existential and the essential in terms of the relationship between psychology and theology. I am interested in the function of the existential and the essential as I adapt them to the interaction between the religious and relational instincts.

26. *The Oxford English Dictionary*, 2d ed., s.v. "religion."

27. The term "God" can be understood here in the Christian theological framework. However, the emphasis is on the function of the concept of God, that which is believed to be the organizing premise for worldview and meaning.

28. This case material is used with written permission.

29. See van Herik, *Freud on Femininity and Faith*, 152–159, for her discussion of the effects of asymmetrical patterns.

30. This is not to imply that only this framework can accomplish this task. However, this framework is the focus here. And it is a unique framework for its ability to raise critical questions as part of its ongoing methodology. I have not seen evidence that another framework would be able to treat the religious and the relational instincts as thoroughly.

31. A vivid illustration of this is Freud's analysis of the Christian religion and the complex dimensions of illusion he assigned to it. See Freud's *The Future of an Illusion*. See also van Herik's *Freud on Femininity and Faith*, 162–169, for a discussion of Freud's analysis.

32. Fiorenza, *In Memory of Her*, xxi.

33. Fiorenza, *Bread Not Stone*, 149.

34. Fiorenza, *In Memory of Her*, 29–30.

35. Ibid., 350.

36. Fiorenza, *Bread Not Stone*, 88.

37. Sturdivant, *Therapy with Women*, 178.

38. Ibid., 6.

39. Ibid.

40. Ibid.

41. See discussion of the term "pastoral" in Clebsch and Jaekle, *Pastoral Care in Historical Perspective*, 4.

42. Ibid., 8–9.

43. For an excellent discussion of the tension and possibility between science and feminism in the construction of models see Harding, *The Science Question in Feminism*, 243–251.

44. Fiorenza, "The Will to Choose or to Reject," 130.

45. Ibid., 135.

46. Ibid., 130.

47. Ibid.

48. Ibid., 131.

49. Ibid., 132–133.

50. Ibid., 133.

51. Ibid., 135.

52. Kleinman, *Patients and Healers in the Context of Culture,* 41.

53. Janine Roberts, "Setting the Frame: Definition, Functions, and Typology of Rituals," 8.

54. DeMarinis, "A Psychotherapeutic Exploration of Religious Ritual as Mediator of Memory and Meaning," 1.

55. Ibid., 11. For an example of the function of religious dance ritual from Afro-Brazilian Macumba culture in a cross-cultural, psychotherapeutic encounter see my "Movement as Mediator of Meaning."

Bibliography

Browning, Donald S. "Introduction to Pastoral Counseling." In *Clinical Handbook of Pastoral Counseling,* edited by Robert J. Wicks, Richard D. Parsons, and Donald E. Capps. New York: Paulist Press, 1985.

Clebsch, William A., and Charles R. Jaekle. *Pastoral Care in Historical Perspective.* New York: Jason Aronson, 1975.

DeMarinis, Valerie. "Movement as Mediator of Meaning: An Investigation of the Psychological and Spiritual Function of Dance in Religious Ritual." In *Dance as Religious Studies,* edited by Doug Adams and Diane Apostolos-Cappadona. New York: Crossroad, 1990.

———. "A Psychotherapeutic Exploration of Religious Ritual as Mediator of Memory and Meaning: A Clinical Case Presentation of the Therapeutic Efficacy of Incorporating Religious Ritual into Therapy." Paper presented for Visiting Resource Professor Lecture in the Department of Theology, Uppsala University, Uppsala, Sweden, 1992.

Fiorenza, Elisabeth Schüssler. *In Memory of Her: A Feminist Theological Reconstruction of Christian Origins.* New York: Crossroad, 1983.

———. *Bread Not Stone: The Challenge of Feminist Biblical Interpretation.* Boston, Beacon Press, 1984.

———. "The Will to Choose or to Reject: Continuing Our Critical Work." In *Feminist Interpretation of the Bible,* edited by Letty M. Russell. Philadelphia: Westminster Press, 1985.

Freud, Sigmund. *The Future of an Illusion.* In *The Standard Edition of the*

Complete Psychological Works of Sigmund Freud, edited by James Strachey in collaboration with Anna Freud, 21:5–56. London: Hogarth Press and the Institute of Psycho-Analysis, 1927.

Gendlin, Eugene T. "Philosophical Critique of the Concept of Narcissism: The Significance of the Awareness Movement." In *Pathologies of the Modern Self: Postmodern Studies on Narcissism, Schizophrenia, and Depression,* edited by David Michael Levin. New York: New York University Press, 1987.

Gerkin, Charles V. *The Living Document: Re-Visioning Pastoral Counseling in a Hermeneutical Mode.* Nashville: Abingdon Press, 1984.

Gilligan, Carol. *In a Different Voice: Psychological Theory and Women's Development.* Cambridge, Mass.: Harvard University Press, 1982.

Greenspan, Miriam. *A New Approach to Women and Therapy.* New York: McGraw-Hill Book Company, 1983.

Harding, Sandra. *The Science Question in Feminism.* Ithaca: Cornell University Press, 1986.

Harrison, Beverly Wildung. "The Power of Anger in the Work of Love: Christian Ethics for Women and Other Strangers." In *Making the Connections: Essays in Feminist Social Ethics,* edited by Carol S. Robb. Boston: Beacon Press, 1985.

Holifield, E. Brooks. *A History of Pastoral Care in America: From Salvation to Self-Realization.* Nashville: Abingdon Press, 1983.

Homans, Peter. "Toward a Psychology of Religion: By Way of Freud and Tillich." In *The Dialogue Between Theology and Psychology,* edited by Peter Homans. Essays in Divinity, 3. Chicago: University of Chicago Press, 1968.

hooks, bell. *Feminist Theory: From Margin to Center.* Boston: South End Press, 1984.

Jung, C. G. *The Collected Works of C. G. Jung,* VII. Translated by R. F. C. Hull. Bollingen Series, 20. Princeton: Princeton University Press, 1966.

Kleinman, Arthur. *Patients and Healers in the Context of Culture: An Exploration of the Borderland between Anthropology, Medicine, and Psychiatry.* Comparative Studies of Health Systems and Medical Care, 3. Berkeley and Los Angeles: University of California Press, 1980.

McNeill, John T. *A History of the Cure of Souls.* New York: Harper & Row, 1951.

Roberts, Janine. "Setting the Frame: Definition, Function, and Typology of Rituals." In *Rituals in Families and Family Therapy,* edited by Evan Imber-Black, Janine Roberts, and Richard A. Whiting. New York: W. W. Norton and Company, 1988.

Smart, Ninian. *Worldviews: Crosscultural Explorations of Human Beliefs.* New York: Charles Scribner's Sons, 1983.

Sturdivant, Susan. *Therapy with Women: A Feminist Philosophy of Treatment.* New York: Springer Publishing Company, 1980.

Ulanov, Ann, and Barry Ulanov. *Religion and the Unconscious*. Philadelphia: The Westminster Press, 1975.

van Herik, Judith. *Freud on Femininity and Faith*. Berkeley and Los Angeles: University of California Press, 1982.

————. "The Feminist Critique of Classical Psychoanalysis." In *The Challenge of Psychology to Faith*, edited by Steven Kepnes and David Tracy. Edinburgh: T. & T. Clark, 1982.

Wehr, Demaris. "Religious and Social Dimensions of Jung's Concept of the Archetype: A Feminist Perspective." In *Feminist Archetypal Theory: Interdisciplinary Re-visions of Jungian Thought*, edited by Estella Lauter and Carol Schreier Rupprecht. Knoxville: University of Tennessee Press, 1985.

Wulff, Henrik R., Stig Andur Pedersen, and Raben Rosenberg. *Philosophy of Medicine: An Introduction*. Oxford: Blackwell Scientific Publications, 1986.